Easy Sausage Making

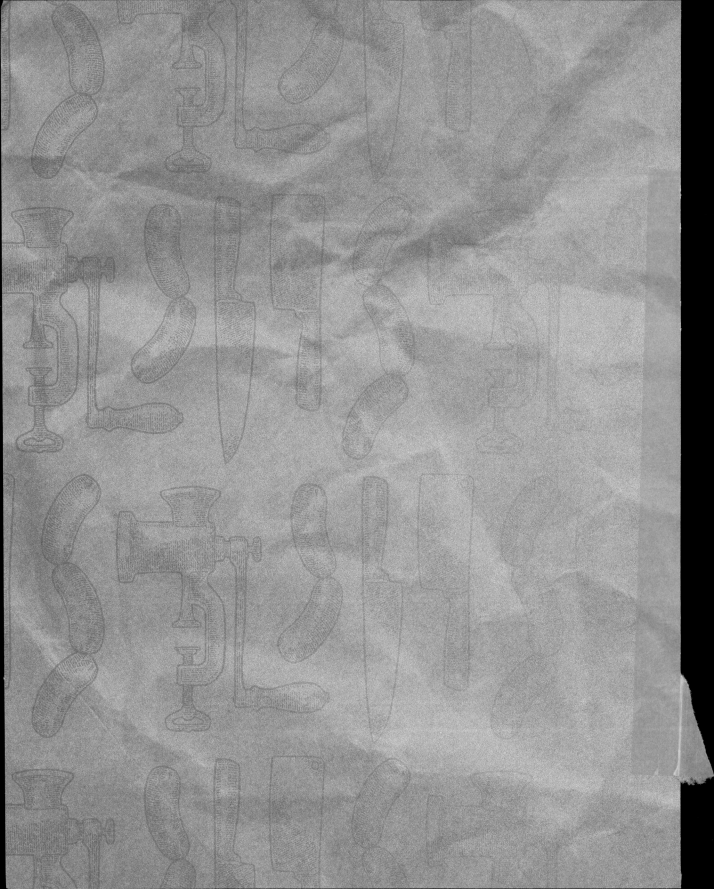

EASY SAUSAGE MAKING

ESSENTIAL TECHNIQUES and RECIPES to MASTER MAKING SAUSAGES at HOME

WILL BUDIAMAN
Foreword by Curt Clingman

ROCKRIDGE
PRESS

Photography © Christopher Testani, cover; Thorsten kleine Holthaus/Stockfood, p. vi; Jen Siska, food styling by Curt Clingman, pp. viii, xii, 26-34 & 176; Nadine Greeff/Stocksy, p. 38; Dan Jones/Stockfood, p. 90 & back cover.

Illustrations © MoreVector/Shutterstock.com, pp. ii, 3, 11 & 21; Tom Bingham, p. 19.

ISBN: Print 978-1-62315-850-7 | eBook 978-1-64152-010-2

This book is dedicated to the butchers, ranchers, and farmers who continue to advance the craft of sausage making.

Contents

Foreword

AFTER THE BUDDING COOK DISCOVERS THAT THEY HAVE AN AFFINITY
for executing a recipe—whether it is as a kid baking their first batch of cookies, an adult
making a nourishing pot of soup, or an adventurous foodie experimenting with baking
their own bread—they often find themselves wanting to add more to their culinary skill
set. For home cooks who are also carnivores, I always strongly suggest adding homemade
sausage to their repertoire. It may seem daunting, but it is easier than you think!

Making sausage is a skill that requires a good teacher and simple instructions. Luckily,
Will Budiaman's *Easy Sausage Making* is the perfect book to use when starting. Under his
guidance, the satisfaction of making delicious sausage for yourself, often with little more
than a handful of well-chosen ingredients, comes alive as you begin to understand the
time-honored process that can't be duplicated by mass production. It will bring you happy
results that fuel your sense of pride and accomplishment. The people you cook for will
be happy, too. All the while, you're building intuition step by step as you work through
these recipes.

Will encourages you to experiment, but please use his guidelines throughout the text
to ensure success. Also, be sure to take notes and critique your work. This is an important
step, not just of the sausage-making process, but for improving your skills as a chef overall.

Will discusses using only the highest-quality meats. This is critical—enough cannot
be said about the meat that you start with. Healthy animals help us produce healthy food.
Find a high-quality butcher in your area, ideally one who is sourcing from people they
know personally.

I especially appreciate the depth of research that has been put into *Easy Sausage
Making*. Most of the cultures of the world have some version of sausage in their cuisine.
Will covers a great deal of ground in this book. As you work through the recipes, you will
develop a repertoire that deepens as you go along. By the end, you should find yourself
starting to innately feel and understand what is happening in the mixing bowl.

Easy Sausage Making will pull you into a world that is slipping away. Producing tangible
goods with our own hands is no longer the norm. The satisfaction that you'll experience
from using a small amount of ingredients to make something delicious is a buzz that will
drive you forward. Don't be surprised if you find yourself daydreaming about the next
batch during your sausage-making journey.

Curt Clingman
Chef, consultant, and Chez Panisse alum

Introduction

IT WAS HOT. NOT HOT THE WAY RESTAURANT KITCHENS NORMALLY ARE, but really hot—the kind of day where chefs think of creative places to put cornstarch for a bit of relief. Summer had definitely arrived in New York, with all its merciless humidity. It was also cramped: there were eight of us jostling about in a space no bigger than a one-car garage. If you bent over to check on the oven at the wrong time, you could send a plateful of freshly fried Gorgonzola croquettes into someone's face. And to top it all off, the new chef and I were not getting along. Which was why it was a relief when he sent me away to go make some sausage.

"Go down to pastry and make some *merguez*!" he bellowed.

"What's the recipe?" I asked.

"I don't like the one we have." No surprise there. He didn't like the way we'd been doing a lot of things. "Figure out a new one. There's some lamb in the walk-in fridge."

I was working at a well-loved Mediterranean restaurant located in the trendy NoHo neighborhood of Manhattan. It began decades ago as a local joint, but had turned into a celebrity hangout. The customers expected their favorite menu items to never change. Well, change was coming, starting with the sausage.

I went downstairs into the relative cool and quiet of the basement, where all the ingredients were kept. There was a separate kitchen for our pastry chefs to make dough for fresh pasta and desserts. The other chefs weren't in, so I had the whole space to myself. First, I set up a huge bath of ice water. Next, I searched for all the pieces for the meat grinder and sausage stuffer, and chilled them after I located them. Keeping things cold is rule number one of sausage making. After I gathered the lamb, the casings, and all the spices, all the equipment was nice and cold, and ready to be assembled.

And then I drew a blank.

My introduction to sausage making had been in culinary school, where I'd been taught about food safety, the equipment I'd likely encounter and how to operate it, and the whole process from start to finish—from grinding whole cuts of meat to properly twisting off links. *But we were always given the recipes.* The recipes were only meant to illustrate the techniques, and coming up with my own was clearly going to involve some trial and error.

It actually turned out to be a lot of fun, affording me the chance to exercise some creativity, which was what drew me to cooking in the first place. I thought about merguez I'd tasted before in different places, and considered what I liked most about each one. This helped me come up with a blend of spices I used to season the meat—the key to making great merguez. When I finished my first batch, I felt like I'd really accomplished something special. And since then, I've been hooked.

This book is for beginners. Which is why, in writing it, I've tried to think of all the things I would have liked to know before that pivotal day. So, if you've never made sausage before (but have eaten plenty of it) and you've been wondering how it's done, you've come to the right place. It's not as difficult as you might think.

This book is divided into three parts. Part 1 begins with a brief overview of how the art and craft of sausage making originated, how it has evolved, and the different types of sausage that are available. You'll then learn about the tools of the trade and all the ingredients you'll need, followed by a detailed tutorial on how to make your first batch of sausage.

In Part 2, you'll find recipes organized by region, with a brief introduction about each. Once you've made a few batches, it's time to turn to Part 3, where you'll find creative recipes that make good use of all that delicious, juicy meat. And perhaps after making your first few batches of sausage, you'll have some colorful stories to pass on, too—along with some recipes of your own.

PART 1

SAUSAGE MAKING 101

ALL ABOUT SAUSAGE

CH. 1

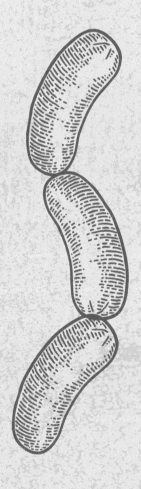

A sausage, in its most basic form, is meat and fat ground together and mixed with salt and other seasonings. In its most familiar form, it's stuffed into a casing, but a sausage is still a sausage even when it's just formed into a patty. From that basic definition, countless varieties have been created all around the world. There are many ways to customize the flavor and texture of sausage to suit your tastes. Just about any kind of meat, poultry, game, or seafood can be used. You can use different cuts of meat from the same animal, or combine cuts from different animals. You can vary the amount of fat to play with richness, consistency, and moisture. You can do the same with dry and wet ingredients, and herbs and spices open up even more possibilities. Between all these choices lie the magical, hard-won, and lucky combinations that brought the traditional, the exotic, the popular, and the downright quirky sausages into existence. And then of course, there are your very own creations.

A Brief History of Sausage Making

Long before the advent of refrigeration, sausage making arose as a solution to a prevalent problem: how to preserve the meat and organs from a slaughtered animal. But that actually wasn't the most pressing problem. In fact, the very first issue to figure out was what to do with all the blood—the part of the animal with the shortest shelf life—which is probably why nearly every sausage-making culture today has some form of blood sausage.

It's hard to pinpoint exactly when sausage was first made, but the domestication of pigs certainly played a big role. Why pigs? Because they fattened quickly on a wide variety of feeds, offering an easy source of tasty meat. The earliest evidence of domestication of pigs dates back to 5000 BCE in Egypt and China, but it wasn't long before pigs were common in Europe and beyond. Their meat—heavily salted and turned into sausage—kept well, making it essential food for the armies of Ancient Greece and Rome. Later on, the medieval period saw the rise of several varieties that are still with us today, such as bologna, frankfurter, and Vienna sausage. And when the Age of Exploration led to encounters with the peoples of the New World, sausage making was discovered here, too. The Cree Indian tribe, for example, made giant sausages called *pemmican*, filled with venison, bone marrow, and berries.

Today, sausage making has undergone a promising revival. After a decades-long run of commercialization and commoditization, sausages are finally getting back to their roots. Thanks to the hard work of butchers, chefs, and farmers, a return to an artisanal approach is taking place. It's now easier than ever to find sausages made by people who can look you in the eye from across the counter and tell you with pride exactly what's in each one.

Sausage Varieties

If you've never done something before, it makes sense to start at the very beginning. Which is why the recipes in this book focus only on fresh sausages. Fresh sausage is the foundation. From there, you can take sausage making in entirely new directions, whether cooking, curing, cold smoking, or barbecuing. Each of these topics could fill its own book, and if you're interested in any of them, I wholeheartedly encourage you to delve deeper. This book focuses on fresh sausages because they are the ideal point of entry for sausage making. So, let's get started on our sausage-making journey.

FRESH SAUSAGE

Fresh sausage is just that—sausage that has been made from freshly ground meat and left raw. It must be cooked before it can be consumed. It can be shaped into patties and fried, or stuffed into casings and then poached, grilled, pan-fried, baked, or steamed. Famous examples that we will cover include Bratwurst (page 59), Pork Breakfast Sausage (page 42), and Sweet Italian Sausage (page 77).

COOKED SAUSAGE

Cooked sausages are ready to eat—that is, they can be eaten without any further cooking. There are two main kinds of cooked sausage: those where the meat is cooked before being stuffed into casings, and those where meat is stuffed raw into casings and then boiled, baked, or smoked before being chilled (essentially, a fresh sausage that is cooked and chilled). Though both are ready to eat, they are often reheated before being served. Boudin is a fine example of the cooked, and the all-American hot dog is a classic example of the raw.

SMOKED SAUSAGE

Smoked sausage is a type of cooked sausage, and there are many popular varieties. Some examples you're probably familiar with include andouille, Texas hot links, and Portuguese linguiça. There's an important distinction to be made here between "cold smoking" and "hot smoking." When people talk about "smoking" a sausage, they generally mean hot smoking or barbecuing, which happens at a minimum temperature of 200°F. At that temperature, smoke not only flavors the meat but also cooks it. Below 200°F, you're curing the meat instead of cooking it. That's a technique sometimes applied to dried sausage, which is the next kind we will discuss.

DRIED SAUSAGE

The most famous type of dried sausage is salami. Dried sausage keeps for a very long time. Making dried sausage requires curing salts or sodium nitrite. These are also known as "pink salt," named for the artificial rosy color they are given so they are not confused with common table salt. But they don't just give the meat beautiful color. They're also responsible for imbuing it with unique flavor, and, most importantly, inhibiting the growth of foodborne pathogens, allowing these sausages to simply be hung up and air-dried.

SPECIALTY MEATS

If you're truly curious about nose-to-tail cooking, this is the category that includes blood sausage, liver sausage, fermented sausage, and headcheese (a gelatinous loaf or link made traditionally from a boiled pig's head). All these delicacies require a great deal of preparation, and originated out of the desire to use every part of the animal.

Regional Flavors and Styles

The sheer diversity of sausages from around the world is astounding. Here is a brief overview from each region.

AMERICAN SAUSAGES

America's sausage offerings have been shaped by the fact that it has always been a country of immigrants. Each wave of immigration has brought with it fascinating food traditions. British, Irish, French, Spanish, Italian, Portuguese, German, Dutch, Swedish, Polish, Chinese, Mexican, Greek, and other cultures have all left their mark and continue to do so today. The classic American breakfast sausage, redolent with sage and black pepper? This comes from Britain. The even more ubiquitous hot dog? It has its origins in Germany, where it still goes by the name of the town where it originated: the frankfurter. Andouille? France. Sweet fennel sausage? Italy. Often, after coming to America, each group took their recipes and adapted them to local ingredients, creating entirely new sausages, like chaurice and Cajun boudin blanc. See chapter 4 for classic and modern American sausage recipes.

GERMAN AND POLISH SAUSAGES

Brats are probably the first things that come to mind when you think of German sausage, but there are also many more varieties. In addition to bratwurst, there's bockwurst, weisswurst, teewurst, mettwurst, blutwurst, and knackwurst—just to name a few. There are a few common threads, though, for all of these. First of all, "wurst" simply means "sausage." Second, pork, beef, and veal are loved in equal measure, and many sausages are some combination of the three. Third and last, most German sausage is cold smoked. The chilly, wet climate means that air-drying sausage isn't a practical option.

There's a similar narrative in Poland. Its climate is similar to Germany's: therefore, many Polish sausages are also smoked. Pork is the most popular protein used, but sometimes there's a little beef or lamb in the mix. The Polish sausage that you're probably familiar with is kielbasa: an all-pork variety that is seasoned with salt, pepper, garlic, and perhaps some marjoram. But in Polish, "kielbasa" actually just means "sausage." In chapter 5 we cover the sausages from both of these countries.

BRITISH AND IRISH SAUSAGES

When it comes to British and Irish sausages, it's the classic pub banger that takes top prize. Bangers and mash—pork sausages paired with mashed potatoes—are the quintessential comfort food. One colorful explanation for their name is that they used to *explode* when cooked, owing to the amount of water added as filler. (Don't worry, our Classic Pub Bangers on page 64 won't explode!)

Blood pudding is arguably the British Isles' other best-known contribution to sausage making. Not a pudding at all in the American sense, blood pudding is a sausage made with pork blood and oats, seasoned with mace, and studded with onion. No English or Irish breakfast is complete without one, and every region proudly touts its own version.

Still, there's so much more to it than pub bangers and blood pudding. In fact, there are more than 400 varieties—most of which are made with pork—between the two countries. Turn to chapter 6 for some great recipes.

MEDITERRANEAN SAUSAGES

Capturing the sheer diversity of the Mediterranean, a region encompassing the Iberian Peninsula, North Africa, Italy, and Greece, is a challenge, but it's also what makes it one of the most exciting sausage-producing regions.

Spain and Portugal are known for paprika-spiked pork sausages, such as chorizo (or chouriço) and linguiça. In Italy, pork also reigns supreme, and it's used to make an impressive variety of sausages, from fresh Tuscan farmhouse links, to hot Calabrian salami. Game meats like wild boar also figure prominently. In North Africa and Greece, lamb and beef are popular choices for cultural and geographical reasons, where they're used to make merguez and loukanika.

The mild, dry climate makes it practical to air-dry sausage, which is why the Mediterranean is home to so many varieties of cured, unsmoked sausage.

If you're ready to journey around the Mediterranean, turn to chapter 7 for recipes.

BEYOND THE WEST SAUSAGES

Virtually any society that has relied on animals as a part of its diet has turned to sausage making to make use of every morsel. Some traditions followed patterns of colonization. Locales as far-flung as the Philippines, Mexico, and the Caribbean, for instance, all have some form of longanisa, a Spanish pork sausage. The common thread is an adaptation of the recipes to the climate—hotter and more humid than Europe—resulting in the use of acidic ingredients, chiles, and hot spices to maximize longevity.

In other cultures, sausage-making recipes arose independently, in forms that we might not immediately recognize as sausage. One example is Otak-Otak (page 86), a fermented Indonesian sausage made by wrapping fish paste in banana leaves, then steaming them. Seafood sausages are prevalent throughout Southeast Asia.

In chapter 8, I offer you a brief but fascinating glimpse into the sausage-making traditions of the rest of the world.

Why You'll Love Making Your Own Sausage

Besides offering the chance to connect with an age-old tradition, making your own sausage has a number of appealing advantages over buying sausage at the store, all of which come down to this simple fact: When you make your own sausage, you can control exactly what goes in it and, perhaps just as important, what doesn't go in it.

- **Eliminate additives and fillers:** Though the state of sausage manufacturing has improved considerably over the past decade, many commercially produced varieties still incorporate substances that do everything from "improving" flavor to extending shelf life. These are all done with one objective in mind: to help producers cut down on costs and make more money. You don't need all that MSG, liquid smoke, artificial flavoring, extra salt, or retained water to add flavor to your creations. And the best part: If you learn how to make your own sausage, you won't need to pay for them anymore.

- **Bring your own flair:** What fun would all this be if it were just about all the bad things you'd be leaving out? Just as important are all the ingredients you'll get to put in that commercial producers deem too niche or expensive. Whole spices, fresh herbs, nuts, eggs, and cheese add vibrant flavor and exciting texture to your sausages.

- **Control the amount of fat:** Fatty meat is cheaper than lean meat and, in accordance with USDA regulations, producers can incorporate up to 50 percent fat by weight into sausage. But you certainly don't need all that fat to make a scrumptious sausage, and now that you know, you probably don't want to eat it. I cover this in depth in the Meat-to-Fat Ratio section in this chapter (page 16).

- **Decide which cuts make the cut:** Though the original spirit of sausage making was to make economical use of every part of the animal, these days some commercial producers might be taking things a bit too far. Just what part of the pig *is* in that dirty water hot dog, anyway? Never mind, don't answer that. Instead of wondering, you can take matters into your own hands and start with whole cuts. Tell your butcher you want responsibly raised pork butt. (Fun fact: Pork butt doesn't actually come from the rear end of the animal but from the upper part of the shoulder and the front leg.)

Making your own sausage is all about customizing and controlling what goes into it. Ready to embark on your sausage-making adventure around the world? It begins right in your own kitchen. Read on to learn about how to get properly prepared for your journey, what equipment to buy, and how to navigate the butcher's counter and stock your pantry.

IN THE KITCHEN

CH. 2

Now that I've whetted your appetite for sausage, it's time to get to the practical stuff and talk about what you'll need to get started. We'll run through all the essential ingredients—talking about meats, casings, herbs, spices, and anything else you'll need to stock your pantry and refrigerator. We'll also talk about all the key equipment you'll need, discussing the pros and cons of the different tools available on the market so that you can make an informed decision about what best suits your needs and budget.

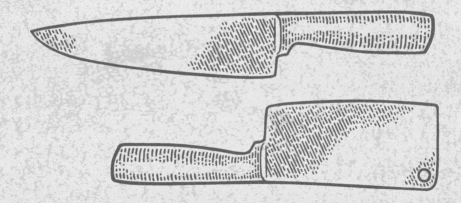

The Ingredients

It's time to do a little shopping. (Okay, it might actually be quite a bit of shopping.) Don't worry, I am going to review every ingredient and how to buy and select each one. Here's what you'll want to put on your list.

MEATS

Pork

Pork butt, also known as Boston butt, is what we use throughout the book for sausages containing pork. It has the perfect amount of fat at about 25 to 30 percent, requires little preparation for grinding, and is readily available and economical.

Beef and Veal

Beef chuck, with its deeply meaty flavor and richness, is a fine choice for making hamburgers, and that makes it great for making fresh sausage, too. It's not expensive and, like pork butt, it has nearly the right amount of fat at 20 percent. As for veal, I like the shoulder for its tenderness and flavor.

Poultry

The thigh is the best cut from any bird for making sausage. On a chicken, for example, it's the fattiest part. And since poultry is so lean compared to pork, beef, or lamb, you want the fattiest part you can find. Skin-on cuts, if you can find them, will make your life a bit easier: they have 20 percent fat, whereas skinless cuts have about 5 percent fat, so you won't have to add much more. Avoid using breasts; they are too lean and will make for a dry, flavorless sausage.

Lamb

With a fat content of about 20 percent, either lamb shoulder or lamb leg work equally well. To cut down on preparation, look for boneless or butterflied cuts. Most lamb you'll find at the store will be imported from New Zealand or Australia. The animals there are grass-fed, which leads to gamier, leaner meat. On the other hand, American lamb—a bit harder to find and pricier—is grain-fed, leading to milder, fattier meat. Which is better? It's really a matter of preference.

Seafood

It's amazing how virtually all fruits of the sea and other bodies of water can be turned into sausage. Shrimp, squid, crayfish, oyster, even lobster can all serve as the base for delicious sausage. The recipes in this book, however, will focus on the two most popular varieties: shrimp and whitefish.

CASINGS

Okay, so this is where things get real. While I've said this before—sausage shaped into patties and fried is still sausage—if you want to make sausage-shaped sausage, you've got to get your hands on some casings.

Natural

The best kind of casing is "natural." This is the most commonly used kind and comes from the intestines of hogs, sheep, and cows. Not to worry: They're scrupulously cleaned and packed in salt to preserve freshness. When it comes to providing tenderness and that unmistakable "snap" when biting into a sausage, there is no substitute.

Hog casings are a great choice for pork, poultry, and seafood sausages and come in a few different sizes. Small casings are 30 to 32 mm (1 to 1¼ inches), medium casings are 32 to 35 mm (1¼ to 1⅓ inches), and large casings are 35 to 44 mm (1⅓ to 1¾ inches). Medium casings are the perfect all-around choice and are what we will use in the book. Picture the typical Italian sausage and you've got the right idea.

Sheep casings are naturally narrower than hog casings—ranging anywhere from 18 to 28 mm, or ¾ to 1 inch in diameter—and are typically used for sausages containing lamb. They're the classic choice for sausages like merguez. They are more delicate than hog casings and may tear more easily, so working with them does take some practice.

Beef casings are the largest of the three—ranging anywhere from 35 to 126 mm, or 1⅓ to 5 inches—and are typically used for cooked or dried sausages like blood sausage, bologna, and cooked salami. I won't be calling for beef casings in this book, but you'll encounter them if you move on to more advanced sausage making.

Synthetic

However, if you really can't *stomach* the idea of using natural casings (sorry, I just had to), try synthetic casings. Synthetic casings come in two varieties: edible and nonedible. Edible casings are a typical choice for fresh sausages; nonedible casings are reserved for dried and cured sausages like salami. The most readily available edible casings are edible collagen casings, which are made from beef hides. Collagen is a substance that makes up the connective tissue in muscle, and, due to its flexibility, is ideal for making casings.

Regardless of whether you choose natural or synthetic, where do you buy casings and how much do you need? Your local butcher or the meat counter at the supermarket is a good place to start. If you have access to a restaurant supply store, that's also a good place to go. Barring all that, there's always Amazon.com. Casings are sold by the "hank," and a hank is about 300 feet long. Pork casings will hold about 100 to 125 pounds of meat; lamb casings, about 40 to 50. In other words, one hank will last you awhile!

HERBS AND SPICES

For the best flavor, we will use fresh herbs for our sausage recipes. If you don't have fresh herbs, you can substitute dried; just use half the amount. If you're going to use dried herbs, store them away from heat and light in order to preserve their flavor, and throw them out after about six months. The same goes for spices.

When ground, a spice has increased surface area, which means that more of it is exposed to heat, light, and air, causing oxidation and a gradual loss of flavor. Therefore spices, whenever possible, should be bought whole in small amounts and then ground just before using in a coffee grinder. Whole spices can also be toasted more easily than ground because they are less likely to burn. Toasting them intensifies their flavor further, bringing out their essential oils.

When shopping for dried herbs and spices, look for a store that does brisk business. It's more likely to have higher turnover, which means the stuff on the shelf will be fresher. If you can find them, look for brands that use dark glass bottles, which prevent light from diminishing the potency of the product.

As for salt, we use kosher salt throughout this book for its neutral flavor and purity. If you use sea salt, you'll probably need to adjust the amount of salt used in your sausages from the recipes. Fine sea salt may seem saltier than kosher salt because a teaspoon of fine crystals will contain more salt by weight than a teaspoon of kosher salt, and vice versa for coarse sea salt. Where the sea salt was harvested also affects the composition of naturally occurring trace elements, and consequently inpacting the salt's flavor and even color. One last thing: Avoid table salt, which contains iodine.

OTHER ADDITIONS

Vinegars, wines, and grains like bread crumbs and oats are useful additions to the pantry for many traditional sausage recipes. Vinegar, for example, is a key ingredient in Mexican chorizo, while bread crumbs (rusk, if you really want to go on a wild goose chase) are essential for authentic British bangers. More creative recipes might make use of nuts, dried fruit, and fresh produce—truly, the only limitation is your imagination!

The Equipment

Now it's time to shop for some tools. Here's a list of the essential equipment you'll need to get started making your own sausage. You probably have most of these items in your kitchen already, save perhaps for the meat grinder and stuffer.

QUALITY MEATS

A sausage only tastes as good as the meat you put into it. Animals that roam free, forage, and eat what they were meant to eat are happier, which leads to better-tasting meat. If you've ever tasted ham from Spanish hogs raised on acorns, you know it's a far cry from Oscar Mayer. Those that are forced into feedlots, pumped full of antibiotics, and made to live very stressful lives suffer, and so does the quality of the meat.

So, how do you source responsibly raised meat? A good place to start might be your favorite restaurants. Talk to the chefs or managers and ask if they can point you to some purveyors or butchers they like. Farmers' markets are also promising, and reading reviews for butcher shops online is also a good strategy.

Buying organic, antibiotic-free, grass-fed, pasture-raised, or heritage-breed meat can be expensive. As a result, it pays to comparison-shop, keeping an eye on the price per pound. And if you're willing to put a little more work into prep—buying bone-in versus boneless—you can save a bit more money. Butchers are happy to recommend substitutes, too. If a fattier cut is on sale, they should be able to recommend the right amount to mix in with the leaner cut to maintain your meat-to-fat ratio.

KNIVES

Look for a high-quality chef's knife from reputable manufacturers such as Zwilling, J.A. Henckels, or Global knives. There's no need to spend a fortune. Rather, concentrate on taking good care of your knife: Store it in a block rather than loose in a drawer to avoid nicking the blade. Invest in a sharpening steel and use it regularly to maintain your knife's edge.

CUTTING BOARDS

Have at least two on hand: a nonporous one that can be sanitized for trimming raw meat, and another one for prepping fruits, vegetables, and any other ingredients. Boards with rubberized feet, which prevent them from sliding around as you work, can make life in the kitchen a bit easier.

MEAT-TO-FAT RATIO

Fat carries flavor and contributes to the texture and juiciness of sausage. But just how much do you need? The magic number is about 25 to 30 percent by weight, which is what we aim for in this book. Depending on how lean the cut of meat is for a recipe, I may call for pork back fat to be used to achieve this percentage. By comparison, your average super-market sausage can have up to 50 percent fat, while ground beef for hamburgers is usually "80/20," or 80 percent lean and 20 percent fat. Just like with making your own hamburger, though, everyone has their own preference, so do feel free to experiment.

SCALE

It would be slightly disconcerting to find pork butts at a store that all weighed exactly 4 pounds—indeed, as you'll quickly discover, buying whole cuts of meat hardly ever results in a nice round weight number. So, once you get your meat home, you'll need to be able to weigh out the amount you need for the recipe. Look for a scale with at least a 10-pound capacity, just in case you decide to start making larger batches. Digital or analog? That's up to you.

MEASURING CUPS AND SPOONS

Opt for stainless steel over plastic for durability. Look for sets that have ¼-cup, ⅓-cup, ½-cup, and 1-cup measures, as well as ¼-teaspoon, ½-teaspoon, 1-teaspoon, and 1-tablespoon measures. You are going to be doing a lot of different measurements, and it will help to have a robust set.

THERMOMETERS

Ideally, you'll have two different thermometers: one that will allow you to monitor the temperature of the ground meat at surface level, and one that will help you keep an eye on the internal temperature of the meat. For the first task, an infrared thermometer will do nicely. For the second task, look for an instant-read thermometer. To take a reading, insert it into the center of the sausage without piercing it through to the other side.

SPICE GRINDER

Toasting spices whole and grinding them yourself adds depth and complexity to sausage. An electric model makes quick work of grinding whole spices. If you already have a grinder that you use for coffee, make sure to wash the insert thoroughly before and after using.

SHEET PANS

Sheet pans are available in a variety of sizes. They're useful for organizing your workspace and, with their lipped edges, also provide a handy place for your sausage to land as you're filling the casings, especially given that they should land on a wet surface. For our purposes, half sheet pans are best.

WIRE RACKS

Wire racks, designed to fit snugly into sheet pans, are useful for elevating your sausages once they're stuffed into casings and placed in the refrigerator. This promotes air circulation, which helps the meat bind to the casing evenly on all sides, improving texture.

SAUSAGE PRICKER

Air pockets will sometimes form as you're filling casings with ground meat, leaving areas where bacteria can grow. A sausage pricker has three prongs that will poke small holes in the casing to eliminate these pockets.

GRINDER

There are a vast array of grinders to cater to just about anyone's needs and budget. If you're just starting out, you may find an inexpensive, hand-operated grinder completely sufficient. On the other hand, if you're turning into a bit of a sausage-making aficionado, you may want to consider something with a motor. No matter what kind of grinder you buy, it's important to make sure it comes with at least two different-size dies. Dies, or plates, are perforated metal disks that the meat gets pushed through as it's ground. Look for ⅛-inch and ⅜-inch dies, otherwise known as fine and coarse dies. The following are the different kinds so you can figure out which one is best for you.

Hand Grinder

The operation of a typical hand grinder is intuitive: Simply drop cubed pieces of meat into the opening and turn the crank to force the meat through the chamber and out of the die. Selecting one is equally straightforward: Look for heavier steel or cast iron models that will stand the test of time, with a clamp that can attach to the edge of the countertop. Prices range from $25 to $100.

Electric Grinder

An electric grinder follows a similar design, except a motor replaces the crank and saves your arm from pain, especially if you are making many batches. Some come with funnels for stuffing, too. Prices range from $70 to $175.

Food Processor

If you already have a food processor with a strong motor, you can use it to grind small batches of meat for coarse, rustic sausage. It also works for fish or seafood sausages. You'll need to keep a close eye on the temperature, as meat tends to heat up more easily in a food processor. Be careful not to overprocess and turn the meat into a paste. Depending on the model, grinder attachments may also be available. Prices range from $30 to $200.

Mixer Attachment

Meat-grinding attachments are also a popular choice for those who own stand mixers. They often come with funnels as well. Prices range from $60 to $80.

SAUSAGE STUFFER

The sausage stuffer is the only other piece of specialized kitchen equipment you'll need to buy. Keep in mind that the price ranges below are for home equipment. Commercial equipment costs hundreds, and in some cases thousands, of dollars more. But unless you plan to start selling your sausages out of a truck, you'll probably find something below to suit your needs.

Hand Stuffer

A hand stuffer is cheap and effective for small batches. These straight plastic tubes are generally about 5 inches long and come in different diameters to accommodate the size of the casing. Prices range from $2 to $5.

Push Stuffer

Push stuffers feature a plunger that pushes ground meat into a curved cylinder, ending in a funnel. To stuff meat into casings, you place the meat inside the cylinder, then push down on the handle attached to the plunger. It's a little easier to use than a hand stuffer, but it will still require a fair amount of elbow grease. Prices range from $50 to $75.

Crank Stuffer

Crank stuffers are a lot easier to use than push stuffers because they a offer mechanical advantage by utilizing leverage to help the user stuff sausages easily. They typically have a vertical design: The meat is loaded into a cylinder, and a large, crank-operated plunger pushes it down and forces it out the funnel. Prices range from $50 to $150.

Mixer Attachment

Manufacturers often bundle sausage-stuffing attachments for stand mixers together with grinder attachments. Ideally, the attachment will come with funnels in a few different sizes. Prices range from $10 to $30.

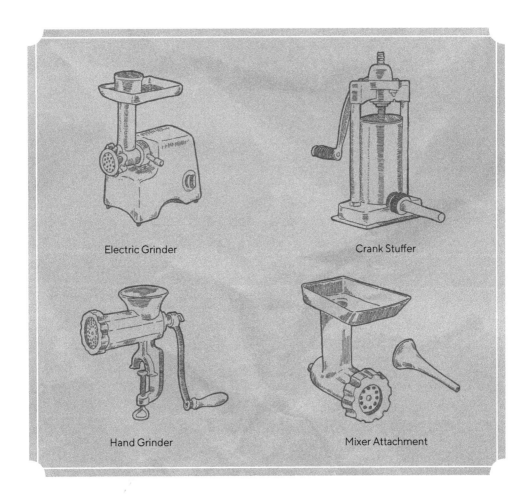

Electric Grinder

Crank Stuffer

Hand Grinder

Mixer Attachment

YOUR
FIRST
BATCH

CH. 3

At last, you've got everything you need to start making sausage. In this chapter, we'll explore the step-by-step process for making every kind of fresh sausage. I'll also walk you through common pitfalls that may arise and how to deal with them. Finally, you will learn the different ways you can cook your delicious batch of fresh sausage. But first, we'll begin with an important discussion about safety consider-ations and general best practices.

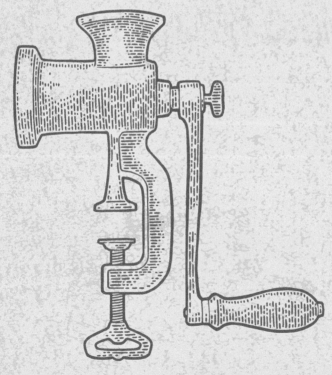

Best Practices

It's time to talk about the best practices for safe home sausage making. Having a successful sausage-making experience comes down to two things: avoiding harmful bacteria and cross-contamination. Not all bacteria are bad. We need some to help us digest our food, while others are responsible for making food taste delicious. But there are also harmful ones, known as pathogens, which cause foodborne illnesses. Cooking food properly destroys all bacteria, but only if it's been handled carefully before cooking. This means staying out of the "danger zone," temperatures between 40°F and 140°F at which bacteria thrive. At room temperature, they multiply very quickly—doubling in numbers every 20 minutes. While it's impossible to stop them from multiplying completely, you can slow them to a manageable pace. Refrigerated, bacteria numbers double only every 38 hours.

What about cross-contamination? That's what happens when raw meat or poultry comes in contact with clean ingredients or cooked food, allowing pathogens to cross over and multiply there. So please read this next part carefully, and follow these tips, for safety's sake.

- **Shop like a pro:** Place meats in a separate bag from produce and limit their time outside of refrigeration by shopping for them last and putting them away in your refrigerator right when you get home.

- **Time is of the essence:** Ideally, use meat to make sausage on the same day you purchased it. If not, use it within 36 hours. Avoid grinding the meat until you need it, since grinding whole cuts of meat increases their surface area. This yields more space on which bacteria can multiply, causing bacteria from the surface of the meat to spread to the interior.

- **Keep your workspace clean:** Clean grinding and stuffing equipment with boiling water and air-dry at room temperature. Clean knives and all surfaces that come in contact with food using a mild bleach solution and let them stand for several minutes before rinsing them with water. Pay special attention to porous surfaces such as wooden cutting boards, which are notorious for harboring bacteria.

- **Chill grinding and mixing equipment:** Keep meat and equipment below 40°F throughout the sausage-making process. That means putting meat, equipment, or both back in the refrigerator if it heats up too much during grinding. Keep the kitchen at 70°F or below.

- **Organize:** Clear your work surface of any clutter. Before you even start grinding, perform all necessary knifework (such as cutting or chopping produce) and measure out any wet or dry ingredients. Staying organized helps you work fast, which keeps your meat cool.

- **Stay sharp:** A dull blade reduces your grinder's effectiveness, making it work harder to cut your meat and generating unwanted heat. If you have sandpaper, safety gloves, safety glasses, and a lot of time to spare, you can do it yourself. But your best bet is to take it (along with the die) to a professional knife sharpener.

Basic Technique—At a Glance

Here is a basic overview of the sausage making process from start to finish. This guide is meant to be a quick reference. You may wish to glance at it as you make the recipes in Part 2. A more detailed step-by-step tutorial of the techniques, illustrated by an easy-to-follow sausage recipe, follows.

Step 1 **Clean Your Casings and Chill Your Tools.** Rinse your casings under warm running water for at least 30 seconds. Inspect the casings for any leaks, then soak them in warm water for at least 1 hour. Meanwhile, place a metal mixing bowl and all the parts for your grinder and stuffer in the refrigerator to chill.

Step 2 **Prepare Your Ingredients.** Trim away and discard any sinew, connective tissue, bones, or excess fat from your meat, then cut the meat into roughly 1-inch cubes. Place the meat in the freezer for at least 1 hour. Measure out any wet or dry ingredients. Cut or chop any fresh produce as directed.

Step 3 **Grind the Meat.** Assemble your grinder according to the manufacturer's directions. Position the mixing bowl next to the grinder and turn on the grinder. Feed the meat into the grinder a few cubes at a time, gently using the plunger to push it through. Never use your hands. Once all of the meat has been ground, turn off the grinder.

Step 4 **Mix in Any Wet and Dry Ingredients.** Add any wet and dry ingredients to the bowl, then knead the mixture for at least 5 minutes with clean, dry hands.

Step 5 **Cook and Taste the Meat.** Heat a small pan over low heat. Add a touch of oil or cooking spray. Form a small patty of meat and add it to the pan. Cook the patty until cooked through but not browned. Remove the patty from the heat and let it cool. Once it is cool enough to handle, taste the cooked patty and adjust the seasoning on the remaining meat as needed. Place the meat in the refrigerator.

Step 6 **Stuff the Casing.** Lubricate the horn of the stuffer and dampen your work surface. Slide the entire casing onto the horn. Remove the meat from the refrigerator. Turn on the stuffer (if electric) and push the meat through it. Once the meat starts to emerge from the horn, stop. Pull off several inches of the casing, and tie the end off in a knot. Resume stuffing until all of the meat has been used. Pull any remaining casing off the horn and tie another knot at this end. Cut off and reserve any extra casing for your next batch.

Step 7 **Inspect the Sausage.** Look for any air bubbles under the casing and prick them with a sausage pricker to remove air pockets.

Step 8 **Twist Off Links.** Measure off your desired length and twist the sausage several times to form your first link. Measure again, and twist in the opposite direction several times to form your second link. Continue, alternating directions, until the entire length has been twisted into links.

Step 9 **Let the Flavors Meld.** Hang the sausages in the refrigerator or coil up and place them on a wire rack set over a sheet pan in the refrigerator overnight.

Recipe Tutorial: Your First Sausage

This in-depth tutorial will enable you to practice the key techniques I have just outlined. Here, you'll learn not just what to do, but why. This section illustrates the techniques with the recipe for Sweet Italian Sausage, a beginner-friendly classic. To get the most of this section, follow along in the kitchen—after all, the best way to learn is not just to read, but to do.

SWEET ITALIAN SAUSAGE

COARSE AND MILD | YIELD: ABOUT 2 POUNDS

Paired with sweet peppers and simmered in tomato sauce until soft, Sweet Italian Sausage is an Italian-American classic. This version is studded with classic fennel seeds, as well as fresh oregano for an herbaceous accent.

EQUIPMENT
Grinder with the coarse (⅜-inch) die
Stuffer
1 metal mixing bowl
Small pan
Sheet pan
Wire rack

INGREDIENTS
4 feet medium hog casings
2 pounds pork butt
1 tablespoon fennel seeds, toasted
    if desired
1 tablespoon kosher salt
2 teaspoons freshly ground black pepper
1 tablespoon chopped fresh oregano
6 garlic cloves, finely chopped

continued ➡

Step 1 **Clean Your Casings and Chill Your Tools.** Untangle your casings. If using synthetic casings, follow the manufacturer's directions. If using salt-packed casings, gently open one end, and slip it onto your kitchen faucet. Turn on the tap, and let warm water run through the casing for at least 30 seconds. Take note of any sections that leak, and simply cut them out. If using brined casings, skip the rinsing. Measure and cut off at least 4 feet of the casing. It doesn't have to be exact, but it's better to have excess than not enough. Soak the casing in warm water for at least 1 hour. Repack the remaining casings. While the casing is soaking, place a metal mixing bowl and all the parts for your grinder and stuffer in the refrigerator to chill. This will help keep the meat cold as you work with it.

Step 2 **Prepare Your Ingredients.** Trim away and discard any sinew, connective tissue, glands, bits and pieces of bone, and excess fat from your pork butt. Anything you don't want to end up in your sausage has to be removed. Cut the pork butt into roughly 1-inch cubes; the pieces should be small enough to easily fit through the feed tube of your grinder. Place the meat in the freezer for at least 30 minutes or until it firms up and ice crystals form. This will help the meat grind cleanly. Place the fennel seeds, salt and pepper in a bowl, and the oregano and garlic in a separate bowl.

continued

Step 3 **Grind the Meat.** Assemble your grinder according to the manufacturer's directions, using the coarse die. Position the mixing bowl next to the grinder. Turn on the grinder. Drop the meat into the feed tube a few cubes at a time, gently using the plunger to push it through as needed. Never use your hands. The meat should emerge from the grinder looking like spaghetti throughout the process. Once all of the meat has been ground, turn off the grinder.

Step 4 **Mix in the Wet and Dry Ingredients.** Add the fennel seeds, salt, pepper, chopped oregano, and chopped garlic to the bowl of ground meat. Knead the mixture for at least 5 minutes, or until the seasonings are evenly distributed and a piece of the mixture sticks upside down to the palm of your hand. This means that the mixture of protein, fat, and liquid (though there isn't any in this recipe) has emulsified, or incorporated thoroughly. Don't be afraid to put some muscle into it. Pretend you're making fresh dough for pizza or pasta.

continued ➔

Step 5 **Cook and Taste the Meat.** This is a key step. A sausage recipe isn't a baking recipe; it isn't meant to be followed too exactly. The amount of seasoning and other ingredients needed will vary slightly depending on how your meat tastes, and how your meat tastes depends on where it's coming from, what time of year it is, and what the animal has been eating. Heat a small pan over low heat. Add a touch of oil or cooking spray. Form a small patty and add it to the pan. Cook the patty until it is cooked through but not browned. Unlike cooking a steak, you don't want a hard sear. A hard sear initiates something called the Maillard reaction, which results in the formation of new flavor compounds. While this is delicious, it won't give you a realistic idea of what your sausage will taste like. Remove from the heat and let it cool. Once it is cool enough to handle, taste the cooked patty and adjust the seasoning on the remaining meat as needed. Feel free to form a second patty and retest. Just remember not to get carried away or there won't be much left to stuff into the casings! Once you're satisfied, place the meat in the refrigerator while you assemble your stuffer.

Step 6 **Stuff the Casing.** Lubricate the horn of the stuffer with a bit of vegetable oil and dampen your work surface with some water. If you'd rather not wet your kitchen counter, this is where a sheet pan comes in handy; you can use that instead. Slide the entire soaked casing onto the horn, taking care not to create any tears. Position the thumb and forefinger of one hand close to the end of the horn to help guide the casing on straight as you gently roll it up the horn with the other. Remove the meat from the refrigerator. Turn on the stuffer (if electric) and push the meat through the stuffer using the plunger. Once it starts to emerge from the horn, stop. Pull off several inches of the casing, and tie the end off in a knot. Resume stuffing until all of the meat has been used, using your free hand—or this is where a helper can step in—to guide the meat as it fills the casing. It should feel firm to the touch with a slight give, but not hard as a rock. You will develop an intuitive sense of what a sausage should feel like when you begin to make more of it. An overstuffed sausage will burst when twisted into links. Pull any remaining casing off the horn and tie a knot off at this end. Cut off and reserve any extra casing for your next batch.

continued ➡

Step 7 **Inspect the Sausage.** Look for any air bubbles and prick the casing with a sausage pricker. Air bubbles can harbor bacteria, and, equally worrisome, can cause the sausage to explode when cooked.

Step 8 **Twist Off Links.** Measure off your desired length and twist the sausage several times to form your first link. There should be about a ¼- to ½-inch gap of twisted casing between each link. Measure again and twist in the opposite direction several times to form your second link. Continue, alternating directions, until the entire length has been twisted into links. Alternating directions will prevent the sausage from unraveling.

continued ➡

Step 9 **Let the Flavors Meld.** Hang the sausages in the refrigerator or place on a wire rack set over a sheet pan in the refrigerator overnight, to allow the flavors to set and meld. This also allows the meat to bind to the casing, improving texture. Congratulations! You've just made your first batch of sausage.

Troubleshooting

Don't worry if something has gone a bit off track. When you begin making sausage, don't expect to be a professional at it right away. Here is a list of the most common issues that pop up while making sausage with solutions of how to deal with them.

- **The meat coming out of the grinder is starting to smear.** "If it don't look like spaghetti, it ain't gonna be pretty," said a chef I once worked with regarding making sausage. When you're grinding your meat, it should emerge from the grinder as separate strands. If it starts to come out in a giant blob, it's time to stop. First, unplug the grinder (if electric) and check to see if there's any sinew or connective tissue caught in the die or blade. If so, simply clean it off, reassemble the grinder, and see if that does the trick. This will also solve the other potential cause, which is that the blade is not making good contact with the die. If it is not, the blade and die might be heating up too much; try feeding a few ice cubes through to see if that helps. If the meat is still smearing, then the meat and the equipment are too warm and it's time to let things cool down. Take the grinder apart, clean it, and put it back in the refrigerator along with all the meat (both ground and not ground) and wait until the temperature of the meat drops below 40°F. Then you can resume grinding.

- **The casing tears during stuffing.** No sweat. Simply cut out the torn section, tie off a new knot, and resume. You can reuse the meat from the torn section, or just fry it off and have a quick bite.

- **There's leftover casing after stuffing.** Not to worry. Cut off and reserve any clean remaining casing. If you were using salt-packed casings, give it a rinse, pat dry with a clean kitchen towel, then coat with salt, and repack in an airtight container. If you were using brined casing, give it a rinse, then place back in the brine or solution it came in. Salt-packed and brined casings will retain ideal texture in the refrigerator for up to six months. If you were using synthetic casings, pat completely dry and place them in a resealable plastic bag. Do not salt them or allow them to get wet.

- **The texture is too crumbly or dry.** Well, unfortunately, the horse has left the barn on this one. The meat got too warm while it was being ground, which kept it from soaking up moisture and fat. Be sure to keep your meat below 40°F during the grinding process. Staying organized, working efficiently, keeping the kitchen at a temperature of 70°F or below, and keeping ground meat over an ice bath will all help prevent this issue from coming up again. If you're scaling up the recipes to make larger batches, it may help to also keep any unground meat over another ice bath (as larger batches will take longer to process).

Storing Your Sausage

At long last, you've created a batch of sausage. After putting all that work into it, it makes sense to handle it with care, so you don't end up spoiling all your hard work. Fresh sausage should be refrigerated until ready to cook and should be consumed within two to three days. Place the links in a single layer on a sheet pan, and wrap tightly with plastic wrap.

If you plan on freezing them, for best results, place the links in a single layer on a sheet pan lined with parchment paper; make sure they aren't pushed right up against one another, or they'll stick. Freeze them for about an hour, then transfer them to a resealable freezer bag. Fresh sausage will keep in the freezer for up to two months. Thaw them in the refrigerator overnight before cooking. Avoid refreezing thawed sausages, as the texture will suffer.

Cooking Sausage

Ready to savor your sausage? There are a few different methods that you can use to cook fresh sausage. All of them are equally delicious and worth trying. No matter which method you use, remember that the USDA recommends all ground meat should be cooked to an internal temperature of 160°F, which can be determined by inserting an instant-read thermometer into the center of the sausage. Resist the urge to cut into the sausage to determine doneness, as this is inaccurate and also causes juices and flavor to leak out.

GRILLING

Poaching sausages for about 10 to 15 minutes to partially cook them before grilling is recommended. I will cover this technique in depth in the next section. Thoroughly clean the grates of your grill with a wire brush to get rid of any food that may have stuck from a previous session, as well as any debris. Lightly oil the grates with a high-temperature cooking oil. Coating a rolled-up, clean kitchen towel with the oil and rubbing it over the grates makes quick work of this. If using a gas grill, heat on medium until you can see the air above the grates shimmering. If your grill has a lid, lower it to speed the heating process and use less fuel.

If you have a charcoal grill, I recommend using a chimney starter. Chimney starters are relatively inexpensive, make lighting your charcoal much easier, and eliminate the need for lighter fluid. Turn the chimney starter over and stuff the bottom with clean scrap paper. Old newspaper or torn-up paper shopping bags work well. Turn it right-side up and fill it two-thirds full with charcoal. Place it on top of the grates, and light the paper. Once it catches fire, step back and let the charcoal burn until the fire dies out and glowing chunks remain. Wearing heatproof gloves, carefully remove the starter from the grates, lift up the grates, and dump in the charcoal away from your person. Using tongs, arrange the coals so that one side has more charcoals than the other, to create two zones on the grill: a hotter one and a cooler one. Carefully replace the grates and give them a few minutes to heat up.

Lightly oil the sausages. Add the sausages to the grates in a single layer. Cook, turning the sausages occasionally with tongs, until they reach an internal temperature of 160°F. The timing varies depending on the thickness, but typically ranges from 7 to 12 minutes for pre-poached sausage—longer if starting raw. If the grill flares up, on a gas grill, reduce the heat as needed. On a charcoal grill, move the sausages to the cooler section of the grates. This will prevent the outside from drying out before the inside cooks through.

POACHING

Heat a pot of water that is large enough to hold all the sausages over high heat. Once it comes to a simmer, or a temperature of 180°F to 185°F, using tongs, gently lower the sausages into the water. Reduce the heat as needed to maintain the simmer. Do not allow the water to come to a boil at any point. You want to cook the sausages as gently as possible, or the texture will turn tough and dry. Cook until they reach an internal temperature of 160°F. The timing varies depending on the thickness, but usually takes from 15 to 20 minutes.

PANFRYING

Heat a pan that is large enough to hold all the sausages in a single layer over medium-high heat until hot. Work in batches if the biggest pan you have isn't large enough to hold all the sausages at once. If the pan is not nonstick, add a thin layer of oil before proceeding. Add the sausages and cook, turning the sausages occasionally with tongs, until browned all over and the internal temperature reaches 160°F. The timing varies depending on the thickness, but usually ranges from 10 to 15 minutes. If you like, add a thin layer of water toward the end of the cooking process to soften the casings slightly.

Congratulations! You survived sausage boot camp. Now it's time to actually start making some sausage. Turn to Part 2 for the recipes!

FRESH SAUSAGE RECIPES

AMERICAN SAUSAGES

CH. 4

American food traditions are an ever-evolving tapestry of different cultures, and you'll see in this chapter that this is very true of sausage making.

Chaurice is a good example. Now a Cajun favorite, its name is a clue to its origins. It sounds similar to "chorizo," the paprika-laced sausage Spain is known for. But this version hews closer to the Mexican one, with a fiery heat that comes from plenty of cayenne and a savory flavor thanks to its complex blend of spices.

Today, you're just as likely to find sausage being taken in creative new directions as you are to see classics like breakfast sausage and chaurice. Southwestern cuisine, for example, has emerged as its own distinct movement. It weaves all manner of chiles, corn, beans, and zesty spices into colorful and memorable dishes—as captured in the recipe for Southwestern Sausage.

Take a spin through this chapter, where you'll find both classic American favorites and exciting modern inventions.

PORK BREAKFAST SAUSAGE

YIELD: ABOUT 2 POUNDS

Make a batch of these on the weekend, and you might just find yourself waking up early on a weekday—to make breakfast. Sage is the traditional seasoning in this sausage, and we're using a healthy amount of the fresh stuff for an especially vibrant taste and aroma.

EQUIPMENT

Grinder with the coarse (⅜-inch) die
Stuffer
1 metal mixing bowl
Sheet pan
Wire rack

INGREDIENTS

4 feet medium hog casings
2 pounds pork butt, trimmed and cut into
    1-inch cubes
1 tablespoon kosher salt
2 teaspoons freshly ground black pepper
3 tablespoons finely chopped fresh sage

1. Prepare your casings. Refrigerate the mixing bowl and all the grinder and stuffer parts. Freeze the meat, uncovered, for at least 30 minutes.

2. Assemble your grinder. Place the bowl next to the grinder and grind the pork butt into the bowl.

3. Add the salt, pepper, and sage. Knead the mixture for at least 5 minutes.

4. Cook a test piece, taste and adjust the seasonings as preferred, then refrigerate the remaining mix.

5. Assemble your stuffer. Lubricate the horn and slide the casing onto it. Dampen your work surface with water. Stuff the meat into the casing, tying off the open ends at the beginning and end.

6. Prick any air bubbles.

7. Twist off links, alternating directions for each link.

8. Refrigerate overnight, uncovered, on a wire rack set over a sheet pan. Cook or freeze within 3 days.

BEEF BREAKFAST SAUSAGE

YIELD: ABOUT 2¼ POUNDS

This juicy beef version of the American classic is equally delicious. We're sneaking in a little pork fat here for some extra richness, but if you prefer a leaner sausage, feel free to leave it out. Serve with eggs prepared your favorite way, or stir it into a hearty hash.

EQUIPMENT

Grinder with the coarse (⅜-inch) die
Stuffer
1 metal mixing bowl
Sheet pan
Wire rack

INGREDIENTS

4 feet medium hog casings
2 pounds beef chuck, trimmed and cut into
    1-inch cubes
¼ pound pork back fat, cut into ½-inch cubes
1 tablespoon kosher salt
2 teaspoons freshly ground black pepper
3 tablespoons finely chopped fresh sage

1. Prepare your casings. Refrigerate the mixing bowl and all the grinder and stuffer parts. Freeze the meat and fat, uncovered, for at least 30 minutes.

2. Assemble your grinder. Place the bowl next to the grinder and grind the beef chuck and pork back fat into the bowl.

3. Add the salt, pepper, and sage. Knead the mixture for at least 5 minutes.

4. Cook a test piece, taste and adjust the seasonings as preferred, then refrigerate the remaining mix.

5. Assemble your stuffer. Lubricate the horn and slide the casing onto it. Dampen your work surface with water. Stuff the meat into the casing, tying off the open ends at the beginning and end.

6. Prick any air bubbles.

7. Twist off links, alternating directions for each link.

8. Refrigerate overnight, uncovered, on a wire rack set over a sheet pan. Cook or freeze within 3 days.

MAPLE-BACON BREAKFAST SAUSAGE

YIELD: ABOUT 2 POUNDS

This sausage is the perfect companion to a big ol' stack of flapjacks or freshly made waffles. Watch everyone come running into the kitchen as the sweet smell of maple syrup—and yes, bacon—wafts down the hall. Not such a lazy Sunday after all.

EQUIPMENT

Grinder with the coarse (⅜-inch) die
Stuffer
1 metal mixing bowl
Sheet pan
Wire rack

INGREDIENTS

4 feet medium hog casings
2 pounds pork butt, trimmed and cut into
    1-inch cubes
¼ pound thick-cut bacon, cut into
    ¼-inch pieces
1 tablespoon kosher salt
2 teaspoons freshly ground black pepper
6 tablespoons pure maple syrup

1. Prepare your casings. Refrigerate the mixing bowl and all the grinder and stuffer parts. Freeze the meat, uncovered, for at least 30 minutes.

2. Assemble your grinder. Place the bowl next to the grinder and grind the pork butt into the bowl.

3. Add the bacon, salt, pepper, and maple syrup. Knead the mixture for at least 5 minutes.

4. Cook a test piece, taste and adjust the seasonings as preferred, then refrigerate the remaining mix.

5. Assemble your stuffer. Lubricate the horn and slide the casing onto it. Dampen your work surface with water. Stuff the meat into the casing, tying off the open ends at the beginning and end.

6. Prick any air bubbles.

7. Twist off links, alternating directions for each link.

8. Refrigerate overnight, uncovered, on a wire rack set over a sheet pan. Cook or freeze within 3 days.

APPLE-SAGE CHICKEN SAUSAGE

YIELD: ABOUT 2 POUNDS

Looking for a sausage that's on the lighter side? Try this one. Tart green apple and sage are a classic combination for chicken sausage. Fry a batch for Thanksgiving and stir it into the stuffing for a gourmet addition.

EQUIPMENT

Grinder with the fine (⅛-inch) die

Stuffer

1 metal mixing bowl

Sheet pan

Wire rack

INGREDIENTS

4 feet medium hog casings

1½ pounds boneless, skinless chicken thighs, cut into 1-inch cubes

½ pound pork back fat, cut into ½-inch cubes

2 teaspoons kosher salt

2 teaspoons freshly ground white pepper

1 cup finely diced green apple

3 tablespoons finely chopped fresh sage

1. Prepare your casings. Refrigerate the mixing bowl and all the grinder and stuffer parts. Freeze the meat and fat, uncovered, for at least 30 minutes.

2. Assemble your grinder. Place the bowl next to the grinder and grind the chicken thighs and pork back fat into the bowl.

3. Add the salt, pepper, apple, and sage. Knead the mixture for at least 5 minutes.

4. Cook a test piece, taste and adjust the seasonings as preferred, then refrigerate the remaining mix.

5. Assemble your stuffer. Lubricate the horn and slide the casing onto it. Dampen your work surface with water. Stuff the meat into the casing, tying off the open ends at the beginning and end.

6. Prick any air bubbles.

7. Twist off links, alternating directions for each link.

8. Refrigerate overnight, uncovered, on a wire rack set over a sheet pan. Cook or freeze within 3 days.

ROSEMARY-LAMB SAUSAGE

YIELD: ABOUT 2¼ POUNDS

Rosemary's distinct aroma is a refreshing counterpoint to the assertive flavor of lamb. These sausages evoke a classic roast leg of lamb, seasoned with this aromatic herb. Pair with a bold, herbal red wine like Grenache that can stand up to the lamb's gamy taste and mingle well with the rosemary.

EQUIPMENT

Grinder with the coarse (⅜-inch) die

Stuffer

1 metal mixing bowl

Sheet pan

Wire rack

INGREDIENTS

4 feet medium hog casings

2 pounds boneless lamb shoulder or leg, trimmed and cut into 1-inch cubes

¼ pound pork back fat, cut into ½-inch cubes

1 tablespoon kosher salt

2 teaspoons freshly ground black pepper

6 garlic cloves, grated

¼ cup fresh rosemary, finely chopped

1. Prepare your casings. Refrigerate the mixing bowl and all the grinder and stuffer parts. Freeze the meat and fat, uncovered, for at least 30 minutes.

2. Assemble your grinder. Place the bowl next to the grinder and grind the lamb shoulder or leg and pork back fat into the bowl.

3. Add the salt, pepper, garlic, and rosemary. Knead the mixture for at least 5 minutes.

4. Cook a test piece, taste and adjust the seasonings as preferred, then refrigerate the remaining mix.

5. Assemble your stuffer. Lubricate the horn and slide the casing onto it. Dampen your work surface with water. Stuff the meat into the casing, tying off the open ends at the beginning and end.

6. Prick any air bubbles.

7. Twist off links, alternating directions for each link.

8. Refrigerate overnight, uncovered, on a wire rack set over a sheet pan. Cook or freeze within 3 days.

HONEY MUSTARD CHICKEN SAUSAGE

YIELD: ABOUT 2 POUNDS

Dijon mustard lends its sinus-clearing kick to the time-honored pairing of honey and mustard. Here, we use a fine grind to allow the meat to really soak up all the seasonings, resulting in a moist, flavorful sausage.

EQUIPMENT

Grinder with the fine (⅛-inch) die

Stuffer

1 metal mixing bowl

Sheet pan

Wire rack

INGREDIENTS

4 feet medium hog casings

1½ pounds boneless, skinless chicken thighs, cut into 1-inch cubes

½ pound pork back fat, cut into ½-inch cubes

2 teaspoons kosher salt

2 teaspoons freshly ground white pepper

2 tablespoons honey

3 tablespoons Dijon mustard

1. Prepare your casings. Refrigerate the mixing bowl and all the grinder and stuffer parts. Freeze the meat and fat, uncovered, for at least 30 minutes.

2. Assemble your grinder. Place the bowl next to the grinder and grind the chicken thighs and pork back fat into the bowl.

3. Add the salt, pepper, honey, and mustard. Knead the mixture for at least 5 minutes.

4. Cook a test piece, taste and adjust the seasonings as preferred, then refrigerate the remaining mix.

5. Assemble your stuffer. Lubricate the horn and slide the casing onto it. Dampen your work surface with water. Stuff the meat into the casing, tying off the open ends at the beginning and end.

6. Prick any air bubbles.

7. Twist off links, alternating directions for each link.

8. Refrigerate overnight, uncovered, on a wire rack set over a sheet pan. Cook or freeze within 3 days.

SOUTHWESTERN SAUSAGE

YIELD: ABOUT 2 POUNDS

Southwestern cuisine is known for its use of chiles and warming spices like cumin and paprika. Here, we use those ingredients to create a mouthwatering sausage that offers an exciting way to put a creative spin on quesadillas, enchiladas, breakfast tacos, and more.

EQUIPMENT

Grinder with the coarse (⅜-inch) die
Stuffer
1 metal mixing bowl
Sheet pan
Wire rack

INGREDIENTS

4 feet medium hog casings
2 pounds pork butt, trimmed and cut into
    1-inch cubes
1 tablespoon kosher salt
2 teaspoons freshly ground black pepper
2 teaspoons paprika
2 teaspoons ground toasted cumin seeds
2 chipotle peppers in adobo sauce, finely
    chopped, plus 2 tablespoons of the liquid

1. Prepare your casings. Refrigerate the mixing bowl and all the grinder and stuffer parts. Freeze the meat, uncovered, for at least 30 minutes.

2. Assemble your grinder. Place the bowl next to the grinder and grind the pork butt into the bowl.

3. Add the salt, pepper, paprika, cumin, and chipotle peppers with the liquid. Knead the mixture for at least 5 minutes.

4. Cook a test piece, taste and adjust the seasonings as preferred, then refrigerate the remaining mix.

5. Assemble your stuffer. Lubricate the horn and slide the casing onto it. Dampen your work surface with water. Stuff the meat into the casing, tying off the open ends at the beginning and end.

6. Prick any air bubbles.

7. Twist off links, alternating directions for each link.

8. Refrigerate overnight, uncovered, on a wire rack set over a sheet pan. Cook or freeze within 3 days.

BACON CHEESEBURGER SAUSAGE

YIELD: ABOUT 2¼ POUNDS

Ever had trouble deciding between a juicy hot dog and a hearty cheeseburger? Well, now you won't have to. The bacon renders into the surrounding meat as the sausage cooks, permeating it with an irresistible smoky, savory aroma.

EQUIPMENT

Grinder with the coarse (⅜-inch) die
Stuffer
1 metal mixing bowl
Sheet pan
Wire rack

INGREDIENTS

4 feet medium hog casings
2 pounds beef chuck, trimmed and cut into
    1-inch cubes
1 cup grated American or Cheddar cheese
¼ pound thick-cut bacon, cut into
    ¼-inch pieces
2 teaspoons kosher salt
2 teaspoons freshly ground black pepper

1. Prepare your casings. Refrigerate the mixing bowl and all the grinder and stuffer parts. Freeze the meat, uncovered, for at least 30 minutes.

2. Assemble your grinder. Place the bowl next to the grinder and grind the beef chuck into the bowl.

3. Add the cheese, bacon, salt, and pepper. Knead the mixture for at least 5 minutes.

4. Cook a test piece, taste and adjust the seasonings as preferred, then refrigerate the remaining mix.

5. Assemble your stuffer. Lubricate the horn and slide the casing onto it. Dampen your work surface with water. Stuff the meat into the casing, tying off the open ends at the beginning and end.

6. Prick any air bubbles.

7. Twist off links, alternating directions for each link.

8. Refrigerate overnight, uncovered, on a wire rack set over a sheet pan. Cook or freeze within 3 days.

CHAURICE

YIELD: ABOUT 2¼ POUNDS

Chaurice is the Big Easy's answer to Spanish and Mexican chorizo. A healthy dose of cayenne results in its famously formidable heat, while a handful of freshly chopped parsley provides a refreshing contrast to the bold seasonings.

EQUIPMENT

Grinder with the coarse (⅜-inch) die
Stuffer
Medium pan
1 metal mixing bowl
Sheet pan
Wire rack

INGREDIENTS

4 feet medium hog casings
2 pounds pork butt, trimmed and cut into
    1-inch cubes
1 tablespoon butter
2 cups finely diced white or yellow onion
6 garlic cloves, chopped
1 tablespoon kosher salt
2 teaspoons freshly ground black pepper
1 tablespoon paprika
2 teaspoons cayenne pepper
1 teaspoon dried oregano
½ teaspoon ground cinnamon
½ cup chopped flat-leaf parsley

1. Prepare your casings. Refrigerate the mixing bowl and all the grinder and stuffer parts. Freeze the pork butt, uncovered, for at least 30 minutes.

2. In a pan, heat the butter over medium-high heat until melted. Add the onion and garlic. Sauté, stirring occasionally so the garlic doesn't burn, 6 to 7 minutes, or until slightly softened. Remove from the heat and set aside to cool.

3. Assemble your grinder. Place the bowl next to the grinder and grind the pork butt into the bowl.

4. Add the onion-and-garlic mixture, salt, pepper, paprika, cayenne, oregano, cinnamon, and parsley. Knead the mixture for at least 5 minutes.

5. Cook a test piece, taste and adjust the seasonings as preferred, then refrigerate the remaining mix.

6. Assemble your stuffer. Lubricate the horn and slide the casing onto it. Dampen your work surface with water. Stuff the meat into the casing, tying off the open ends at the beginning and end.

7. Prick any air bubbles.

8. Twist off links, alternating directions for each link.

9. Refrigerate overnight, uncovered, on a wire rack set over a sheet pan. Cook or freeze within 3 days.

WHITE CHILI CHICKEN SAUSAGE

YIELD: ABOUT 2 POUNDS

White chili is one of New Mexico's claims to fame. It uses chicken instead of beef or pork and features Hatch chiles—green chiles native to Hatch, New Mexico.

EQUIPMENT

Grinder with the fine (⅛-inch) die

Stuffer

1 metal mixing bowl

Sheet pan

Wire rack

INGREDIENTS

4 feet medium hog casings

1½ pounds boneless, skinless chicken thighs, cut into 1-inch cubes

½ pound pork back fat, cut into ½-inch cubes

2 teaspoons kosher salt

2 teaspoons freshly ground white pepper

2 teaspoons ground toasted coriander seeds

1 teaspoon ground toasted cumin seeds

½ teaspoon cayenne pepper

1 (4-ounce) can diced green Hatch chiles

6 garlic cloves, grated

½ cup dried bread crumbs

1. Prepare your casings. Refrigerate the mixing bowl and all the grinder and stuffer parts. Freeze the meat and fat, uncovered, for at least 30 minutes.

2. Assemble your grinder. Place the bowl next to the grinder and grind the chicken thighs and pork back fat into the bowl.

3. Add the salt, pepper, cumin, coriander, cayenne pepper, chiles, garlic and bread crumbs. Knead the mixture for at least 5 minutes.

4. Cook a test piece, taste and adjust the seasonings as preferred, then refrigerate the remaining mix.

5. Assemble your stuffer. Lubricate the horn and slide the casing onto it. Dampen your work surface with water. Stuff the meat into the casing, tying off the open ends at the beginning and end.

6. Prick any air bubbles.

7. Twist off links, alternating directions for each link.

8. Refrigerate overnight, uncovered, on a wire rack set over a sheet pan. Cook or freeze within 3 days.

BEEF CHILI CON CARNE SAUSAGE

YIELD: ABOUT 2¼ POUNDS

This sausage pays homage to the fiery bowls of red that come from the Lone Star State. Classic cumin and two kinds of chiles impart complex flavor. Give your favorite Tex-Mex dishes a serious kick in the pants with this sausage.

EQUIPMENT

Grinder with the coarse (⅜-inch) die

Stuffer

1 metal mixing bowl

Sheet pan

Wire rack

INGREDIENTS

4 feet medium hog casings

2 pounds beef chuck, trimmed and cut into
    1-inch cubes

¼ pound pork back fat, cut into ½-inch cubes

1 tablespoon kosher salt

2 teaspoons freshly ground black pepper

1 tablespoon ground toasted cumin seeds

2 teaspoons paprika

1 teaspoon ground allspice

3 dried red chiles, such as chiles de árbol,
    toasted and ground

2 chipotle peppers in adobo sauce,
    finely chopped

1. Prepare your casings. Refrigerate the mixing bowl and all the grinder and stuffer parts. Freeze the meat and fat, uncovered, for at least 30 minutes.

2. Assemble your grinder. Place the bowl next to the grinder and grind the beef chuck and pork back fat into the bowl.

3. Add the salt, pepper, cumin, paprika, allspice, chiles, and chipotle peppers. Knead the mixture for at least 5 minutes.

4. Cook a test piece, taste and adjust the seasonings as preferred, then refrigerate the remaining mix.

5. Assemble your stuffer. Lubricate the horn and slide the casing onto it. Dampen your work surface with water. Stuff the meat into the casing, tying off the open ends at the beginning and end.

6. Prick any air bubbles.

7. Twist off links, alternating directions for each link.

8. Refrigerate overnight, uncovered, on a wire rack set over a sheet pan. Cook or freeze within 3 days.

GERMAN & POLISH SAUSAGES

CH. 5

A mind-boggling variety of sausages have come from Northern Europe. Germany alone is home to more than 1,200 varieties. And each kind is a proud symbol of a different region. Weisswurst, a poached white sausage made of veal and pork, comes from Bavaria; bratwurst, a tailgating favorite, is a specialty of Franconia; krakowska, a pork sausage spiced with nutmeg, hails from Krakow, Poland.

Sausages have long been an important part of the cuisines in this region. They are often served with a bit of mustard on the side, alongside zesty sauerkraut, or a with a creamy potato salad. Shredded beets, carrots, and steamed cabbage are also popular accompaniments. Sausages are also often added to hearty stews to lend them some richness—perfect for a frosty winter night. And to wash it all down, a local beer is the traditional choice.

FRESH KIELBASA

YIELD: ABOUT 2 POUNDS

Most kielbasa you'll find at the supermarket—and the best-known variety—is smoked. But this fresh version is delicious in its own right, featuring the exact same seasonings, plus it's easier to make. It's traditionally used in soups.

EQUIPMENT

Grinder with the coarse (⅜-inch) die

Stuffer

1 metal mixing bowl

Sheet pan

Wire rack

INGREDIENTS

4 feet medium hog casings

2 pounds pork butt, trimmed and cut into
    1-inch cubes

1 tablespoon kosher salt

2 teaspoons freshly ground black pepper

2 tablespoons finely chopped fresh marjoram

6 garlic cloves, finely chopped

1. Prepare your casings. Refrigerate the mixing bowl and all the grinder and stuffer parts. Freeze the meat, uncovered, for at least 30 minutes.

2. Assemble your grinder. Place the bowl next to the grinder and grind the pork butt into the bowl.

3. Add the salt, pepper, marjoram, and garlic. Knead the mixture for at least 5 minutes.

4. Cook a test piece, taste and adjust the seasonings as preferred, then refrigerate the remaining mix.

5. Assemble your stuffer. Lubricate the horn and slide the casing onto it. Dampen your work surface with water. Stuff the meat into the casing, tying off the open ends at the beginning and end.

6. Prick any air bubbles.

7. Twist off links, alternating directions for each link.

8. Refrigerate overnight, uncovered, on a wire rack set over a sheet pan. Cook or freeze within 3 days.

GARLIC SAUSAGE

YIELD: ABOUT 2 POUNDS

This type of kielbasa is normally cured, but we make a fresh version here that balances the pungent garlic with aromatic spices. To separate the garlic cloves easily, first peel away the outer layers of skin from the head to expose the cloves. Then place your hands, palm over palm, on top of the garlic and press down with your body weight. Watch the cloves come apart easily.

EQUIPMENT

Grinder with the coarse (⅜-inch) die

Stuffer

1 metal mixing bowl

Sheet pan

Wire rack

INGREDIENTS

4 feet medium hog casings

2 pounds pork butt, trimmed and cut into
    1-inch cubes

1 tablespoon kosher salt

2 teaspoons freshly ground black pepper

1 teaspoon paprika

2 teaspoons ground toasted coriander seeds

2 tablespoons finely chopped fresh marjoram

1 garlic head, finely chopped

1. Prepare your casings. Refrigerate the mixing bowl and all the grinder and stuffer parts. Freeze the meat, uncovered, for at least 30 minutes.

2. Assemble your grinder. Place the bowl next to the grinder and grind the pork butt into the bowl.

3. Add the salt, pepper, paprika, coriander, marjoram, and garlic. Knead the mixture for at least 5 minutes.

4. Cook a test piece, taste and adjust the seasonings as preferred, then refrigerate the remaining mix.

5. Assemble your stuffer. Lubricate the horn and slide the casing onto it. Dampen your work surface with water. Stuff the meat into the casing, tying off the open ends at the beginning and end.

6. Prick any air bubbles.

7. Twist off links, alternating directions for each link.

8. Refrigerate overnight, uncovered, on a wire rack set over a sheet pan. Cook or freeze within 3 days.

BOCKWURST

YIELD: ABOUT 2 POUNDS

Bockwurst is a veal-and-pork sausage that is seasoned with paprika and parsley and typically poached and served with bock beer and sweet mustard. This sausage is best served poached to preserve the fine flavor and texture this sausage is known for.

EQUIPMENT

Grinder with the coarse (⅜-inch) die
Stuffer
1 metal mixing bowl
Sheet pan
Wire rack

INGREDIENTS

4 feet medium hog casings
1 pound veal shoulder, trimmed and cut into
      1-inch cubes
1 pound pork butt, trimmed and cut into
      1-inch cubes
¼ pound pork back fat, cut into ½-inch cubes
1 egg, beaten
1 tablespoon kosher salt
2 teaspoons freshly ground white pepper
2 teaspoons paprika
½ teaspoon freshly grated nutmeg
3 tablespoons finely chopped fresh parsley

1.   Prepare your casings. Refrigerate the mixing bowl and all the grinder and stuffer parts. Freeze the meat, uncovered, for at least 30 minutes.

2.   Assemble your grinder. Place the bowl next to the grinder and grind the veal shoulder, pork butt, and pork back fat into the bowl.

3.   Add the egg, salt, pepper, paprika, nutmeg, and parsley. Knead the mixture for at least 5 minutes.

4.   Cook a test piece, taste and adjust the seasonings as preferred, then refrigerate the remaining mix.

5.   Assemble your stuffer. Lubricate the horn and slide the casing onto it. Dampen your work surface with water. Stuff the meat into the casing, tying off the open ends at the beginning and end.

6.   Prick any air bubbles.

7.   Twist off links, alternating directions for each link.

8.   Refrigerate overnight, uncovered, on a wire rack set over a sheet pan. Cook or freeze within 3 days.

BRATWURST

YIELD: ABOUT 2 POUNDS

After the frankfurter (also known as the hot dog), bratwurst is probably the most famous German sausage—with good reason. They're simply delicious grilled and served in a bun, slathered with mustard.

EQUIPMENT

Grinder with the coarse (⅜-inch) die

Stuffer

1 metal mixing bowl

Sheet pan

Wire rack

INGREDIENTS

4 feet medium hog casings

1 pound pork butt, trimmed and cut into
    1-inch cubes

¾ pound veal shoulder, trimmed and cut into
    1-inch cubes

¼ pound pork back fat, cut into ½-inch cubes

1 tablespoon kosher salt

2 teaspoons freshly ground white pepper

2 teaspoons caraway seeds, toasted

½ teaspoon freshly grated nutmeg

1. Prepare your casings. Refrigerate the mixing bowl and all the grinder and stuffer parts. Freeze the meat and fat, uncovered, for at least 30 minutes.

2. Assemble your grinder. Place the bowl next to the grinder and grind the pork butt, veal shoulder, and pork back fat into the bowl.

3. Add the salt, pepper, caraway seeds, and nutmeg. Knead the mixture for at least 5 minutes.

4. Cook a test piece, taste and adjust the seasonings as preferred, then refrigerate the remaining mix.

5. Assemble your stuffer. Lubricate the horn and slide the casing onto it. Dampen your work surface with water. Stuff the meat into the casing, tying off the open ends at the beginning and end.

6. Prick any air bubbles.

7. Twist off links, alternating directions for each link.

8. Refrigerate overnight, uncovered, on a wire rack set over a sheet pan. Cook or freeze within 3 days.

WEISSWURST

YIELD: ABOUT 2 POUNDS

This specialty of Munich is best served poached. It's simply delicious with a side of sauerkraut and mild mustard, and is typically served for breakfast. Here, we complement the richness of the sausage with a bright accent of some freshly grated lemon zest.

EQUIPMENT

Grinder with the fine (⅛-inch) die
Stuffer
1 metal mixing bowl
Sheet pan
Wire rack

INGREDIENTS

4 feet medium hog casings
1½ pounds veal shoulder, trimmed and cut into
    1-inch cubes
½ pound pork back fat, cut into ½-inch cubes
1 egg, beaten
¾ cup whole milk
1 tablespoon kosher salt
2 teaspoons freshly ground white pepper
3 tablespoons finely chopped fresh parsley
¼ cup finely chopped onion
Zest of 1 lemon, grated

1. Prepare your casings. Refrigerate the mixing bowl and all the grinder and stuffer parts. Freeze the meat and fat, uncovered, for at least 30 minutes.

2. Assemble your grinder. Place the bowl next to the grinder and grind the veal shoulder and pork back fat into the bowl.

3. Add the egg, milk, salt, pepper, parsley, onion, and lemon zest. Knead the mixture for at least 5 minutes.

4. Cook a test piece, taste and adjust the seasonings as preferred, then refrigerate the remaining mix.

5. Assemble your stuffer. Lubricate the horn and slide the casing onto it. Dampen your work surface with water. Stuff the meat into the casing, tying off the open ends at the beginning and end.

6. Prick any air bubbles.

7. Twist off links, alternating directions for each link.

8. Refrigerate overnight, uncovered, on a wire rack set over a sheet pan. Cook or freeze within 3 days.

CURRYWURST 2.0

YIELD: ABOUT 2 POUNDS

No visit to Berlin is complete without trying currywurst, a grilled brat that's dusted with curry powder and served with a generous dollop of ketchup, mayonnaise, or both. I was never a huge fan of sprinkling curry powder on top—it usually gave the sausage a gritty feel—so in this version, I've worked some of my favorite Indian spices right into the meat itself.

EQUIPMENT

Grinder with the coarse (⅜-inch) die
Stuffer
1 metal mixing bowl
Sheet pan
Wire rack

INGREDIENTS

4 feet medium hog casings
1 pound pork butt, trimmed and cut into
    1-inch cubes
¾ pound veal shoulder, trimmed and cut
    into 1-inch cubes
¼ pound pork back fat, cut into ½-inch cubes
1 tablespoon kosher salt
2 teaspoons freshly ground black pepper
2 teaspoons garam masala
1 teaspoon ground toasted coriander seeds
1 teaspoon ground toasted fenugreek seeds
1 teaspoon turmeric
½ teaspoon cayenne pepper

1. Prepare your casings. Refrigerate the mixing bowl and all the grinder and stuffer parts. Freeze the meat and fat, uncovered, for at least 30 minutes.

2. Assemble your grinder. Place the bowl next to the grinder and grind the pork butt, veal shoulder, and pork back fat into the bowl.

3. Add the salt, pepper, garam masala, coriander, fenugreek, turmeric, and cayenne. Knead the mixture for at least 5 minutes.

4. Cook a test piece, taste and adjust the seasonings as preferred, then refrigerate the remaining mix.

5. Assemble your stuffer. Lubricate the horn and slide the casing onto it. Dampen your work surface with water. Stuff the meat into the casing, tying off the open ends at the beginning and end.

6. Prick any air bubbles.

7. Twist off links, alternating directions for each link.

8. Refrigerate overnight, uncovered, on a wire rack set over a sheet pan. Cook or freeze within 3 days.

BRITISH & IRISH SAUSAGES

CH. 6

The iconic American breakfast sausage, seasoned with salt, plenty of black pepper, and sage, has its roots in the British culinary traditions brought over by the first settlers. But take a journey across the pond and it's clear that there's so much more to it than that. Since the Romans first introduced the art of sausage making to the British Isles, more than 400 varieties have been developed—and survive to this day. You're probably familiar with bangers, the pub favorite, and you've probably heard of blood pudding. But Lincolnshire sausage or lorne? Perhaps not. Well then, it's time to dig a little deeper and discover exactly what has made these sausages timeless classics.

CLASSIC PUB BANGERS

YIELD: ABOUT 2¼ POUNDS

Bangers were invented as a way to stretch scanty meat rations during the war—hence the inclusion of bread crumbs. They're named for the popping and hissing sounds they make when fried in a pot or pan.

EQUIPMENT

Grinder with the coarse (⅜-inch) die
Stuffer
1 metal mixing bowl
Sheet pan
Wire rack

INGREDIENTS

6 feet small hog casings
2 pounds pork butt, trimmed and cut into
　　1-inch cubes
1 cup dried bread crumbs
1 tablespoon kosher salt
2 teaspoons freshly ground black pepper
2 tablespoons finely chopped fresh sage
2 teaspoons finely chopped fresh ginger
½ teaspoon freshly grated nutmeg

1. Prepare your casings. Refrigerate the mixing bowl and all the grinder and stuffer parts. Freeze the meat, uncovered, for at least 30 minutes.

2. Assemble your grinder. Place the bowl next to the grinder and grind the pork butt into the bowl.

3. Add the bread crumbs, salt, pepper, sage, ginger, and nutmeg. Knead the mixture for at least 5 minutes.

4. Cook a test piece, taste and adjust the seasonings as preferred, then refrigerate the remaining mix.

5. Assemble your stuffer. Lubricate the horn and slide the casing onto it. Dampen your work surface with water. Stuff the meat into the casing, tying off the open ends at the beginning and end.

6. Prick any air bubbles.

7. Twist off links, alternating directions for each link.

8. Refrigerate overnight, uncovered, on a wire rack set over a sheet pan. Cook or freeze within 3 days.

BEEF BANGERS

YIELD: ABOUT 2¼ POUNDS

Pork is the traditional meat of choice for bangers, but if you're in the mood for something different, try this beef version. A touch of pork fat keeps these pub favorites nice and moist as they're panfried—arguably the best way to cook them.

EQUIPMENT

Grinder with the coarse (⅜-inch) die
Stuffer
1 metal mixing bowl
Sheet pan
Wire rack

INGREDIENTS

6 feet small hog casings
2 pounds beef chuck, trimmed and cut into
    1-inch cubes
¼ pound pork back fat, cut into ½-inch cubes
1 cup dried bread crumbs
1 tablespoon kosher salt
2 teaspoons freshly ground black pepper
2 tablespoons finely chopped fresh sage
2 teaspoons finely chopped fresh ginger
½ teaspoon freshly grated nutmeg

1. Prepare your casings. Refrigerate the mixing bowl and all the grinder and stuffer parts. Freeze the meat and fat, uncovered, for at least 30 minutes.

2. Assemble your grinder. Place the bowl next to the grinder and grind the beef chuck and pork back fat into the bowl.

3. Add the bread crumbs, salt, pepper, sage, ginger, and nutmeg. Knead the mixture for at least 5 minutes.

4. Cook a test piece, taste and adjust the seasonings as preferred, then refrigerate the remaining mix.

5. Assemble your stuffer. Lubricate the horn and slide the casing onto it. Dampen your work surface with water. Stuff the meat into the casing, tying off the open ends at the beginning and end.

6. Prick any air bubbles.

7. Twist off links, alternating directions for each link.

8. Refrigerate overnight, uncovered, on a wire rack set over a sheet pan. Cook or freeze within 3 days.

LINCOLNSHIRE SAUSAGE

YIELD: ABOUT 2¼ POUNDS

Named after the county in east England where it originated, this sausage has its very own annual festival, held every October. It is known for its coarse texture and is traditionally seasoned with sage, which grows abundantly in the region.

EQUIPMENT

Grinder with the coarse (⅜-inch) die
Stuffer
1 metal mixing bowl
Sheet pan
Wire rack

INGREDIENTS

4 feet medium hog casings
2 pounds pork butt, trimmed and cut into
    1-inch cubes
1 cup dried bread crumbs
1 tablespoon kosher salt
2 teaspoons freshly ground black pepper
3 tablespoons finely chopped fresh sage

1. Prepare your casings. Refrigerate the mixing bowl and all the grinder and stuffer parts. Freeze the meat, uncovered, for at least 30 minutes.

2. Assemble your grinder. Place the bowl next to the grinder and grind the pork butt into the bowl.

3. Add the bread crumbs, salt, pepper, and sage. Knead the mixture for at least 5 minutes.

4. Cook a test piece, taste and adjust the seasonings as preferred, then refrigerate the remaining mix.

5. Assemble your stuffer. Lubricate the horn and slide the casing onto it. Dampen your work surface with water. Stuff the meat into the casing, tying off the open ends at the beginning and end.

6. Prick any air bubbles.

7. Twist off links, alternating directions for each link.

8. Refrigerate overnight, uncovered, on a wire rack set over a sheet pan. Cook or freeze within 3 days.

CUMBERLAND SAUSAGE

YIELD: ABOUT 2 POUNDS

Here you can skip the usual step of twisting off links, as this spiced sausage is traditionally sold all coiled up in one great length. The proud heritage of this sausage dates back to the 16th century, when German miners migrated into Cumbria, a county in England.

EQUIPMENT

Grinder with the coarse (⅜-inch) die
Stuffer
1 metal mixing bowl
Sheet pan
Wire rack

INGREDIENTS

4 feet medium hog casings
2 pounds pork butt, trimmed and cut into
    1-inch cubes
1 tablespoon kosher salt
2 teaspoons freshly ground black pepper
1 teaspoon freshly ground white pepper

1. Prepare your casings. Refrigerate the mixing bowl and all the grinder and stuffer parts. Freeze the meat, uncovered, for at least 30 minutes.

2. Assemble your grinder. Place the bowl next to the grinder and grind the pork butt into the bowl.

3. Add the salt, black pepper, and white pepper. Knead the mixture for at least 5 minutes.

4. Cook a test piece, taste and adjust the seasonings as preferred, then refrigerate the remaining mix.

5. Assemble your stuffer. Lubricate the horn and slide the casing onto it. Dampen your work surface with water. Stuff the meat into the casing, tying off the open ends at the beginning and end.

6. Prick any air bubbles.

7. Form the sausage into a spiraled coil.

8. Refrigerate overnight, uncovered, on a wire rack set over a sheet pan. Cook or freeze within 3 days.

LORNE

YIELD: ABOUT 2¼ POUNDS

Lorne is a Scottish specialty, traditionally served with a full breakfast. It is formed into shallow rectangular loaves and sliced, rather than stuffed into casings. Panfry it and serve in a slider-style bun for a quick breakfast on the go.

EQUIPMENT

Grinder with the coarse (⅜-inch) die

Stuffer

1 metal mixing bowl

Sheet pan

Wire rack

INGREDIENTS

2 pounds beef chuck, trimmed and cut into 1-inch cubes

¼ pound pork back fat, cut into ½-inch cubes

1 cup dried bread crumbs

1 tablespoon kosher salt

2 teaspoons freshly ground black pepper

½ teaspoon freshly grated nutmeg

2 teaspoons ground toasted coriander seeds

1. Refrigerate the mixing bowl and all the grinder and stuffer parts. Freeze the meat and fat, uncovered, for at least 30 minutes.

2. Assemble your grinder. Place the bowl next to the grinder, and grind the beef chuck and pork back fat into the bowl.

3. Add the bread crumbs, salt, pepper, nutmeg, and coriander. Knead the mixture for at least 5 minutes.

4. Cook a test piece and taste. Adjust the seasonings as preferred.

5. Spread evenly onto a sheet pan.

6. Refrigerate overnight, covered with wax paper. Slice into rectangular pieces and cook or freeze within 3 days.

TOMATO SAUSAGE

YIELD: ABOUT 2¼ POUNDS

In this British butcher counter favorite, tangy tomato offsets the richness of pork, while bread crumbs (or traditionally, rusk) create an airy texture. For a woodsy accent, we season it all with thyme.

EQUIPMENT

Grinder with the coarse (⅜-inch) die

Stuffer

1 metal mixing bowl

Sheet pan

Wire rack

INGREDIENTS

4 feet medium hog casings

2 pounds pork butt, trimmed and cut into
    1-inch cubes

1 cup dried bread crumbs

1 tablespoon kosher salt

2 teaspoons freshly ground black pepper

2 cups crushed tomatoes

¼ cup finely chopped fresh thyme

1. Prepare your casings. Refrigerate the mixing bowl and all the grinder and stuffer parts. Freeze the meat, uncovered, for at least 30 minutes.

2. Assemble your grinder. Place the bowl next to the grinder and grind the pork butt into the bowl.

3. Add the bread crumbs, salt, pepper, tomatoes, and thyme. Knead the mixture for at least 5 minutes.

4. Cook a test piece, taste and adjust the seasonings as preferred, then refrigerate the remaining mix.

5. Assemble your stuffer. Lubricate the horn and slide the casing onto it. Dampen your work surface with water. Stuff the meat into the casing, tying off the open ends at the beginning and end.

6. Prick any air bubbles.

7. Twist off links, alternating directions for each link.

8. Refrigerate overnight, uncovered, on a wire rack set over a sheet pan. Cook or freeze within 3 days.

MARYLEBONE SAUSAGE

YIELD: ABOUT 2¼ POUNDS

A London high-street classic, the Marylebone (pronounced Mar-lee-bone) sausage is fragrant with herbs and spices. It is named after a well-to-do, tree-lined neighborhood nestled between Hyde Park and Regent's Park, famous for its bustling shops and cafés.

EQUIPMENT

Grinder with the coarse (⅜-inch) die
Stuffer
1 metal mixing bowl
Sheet pan
Wire rack

INGREDIENTS

4 feet medium hog casings
2 pounds pork butt, trimmed, and cut into
    1-inch cubes
1 cup dried bread crumbs
1 tablespoon kosher salt
2 teaspoons freshly ground black pepper
½ teaspoon freshly grated nutmeg
4 teaspoons finely chopped fresh ginger
3 tablespoons chopped fresh sage

1. Prepare your casings. Refrigerate the mixing bowl and all the grinder and stuffer parts. Freeze the meat, uncovered, for at least 30 minutes.

2. Assemble your grinder. Place the bowl next to the grinder and grind the pork butt into the bowl.

3. Add the bread crumbs, salt, pepper, nutmeg, ginger, and sage. Knead the mixture for at least 5 minutes.

4. Cook a test piece, taste and adjust the seasonings as preferred, then refrigerate the remaining mix.

5. Assemble your stuffer. Lubricate the horn and slide the casing onto it. Dampen your work surface with water. Stuff the meat into the casing, tying off the open ends at the beginning and end.

6. Prick any air bubbles.

7. Twist off links, alternating directions for each link.

8. Refrigerate overnight, uncovered, on a wire rack set over a sheet pan. Cook or freeze within 3 days.

MEDITERRANEAN SAUSAGES

CH. 7

Salami and similar cured meats are probably the first things that come to mind when someone mentions Mediterranean sausage. But there are plenty of fresh sausages from the area to excite the enthusiasts, too. Ignoring them would be like taking a trip to Italy and eating *only* pasta—well, maybe there's nothing wrong with that, but there *is* more to Italian food than just pasta and pizza. So get ready to take a whirlwind tour through the region: from the Iberian Peninsula, across the French countryside, up into the rolling hills of Italy, and finally over to the storied Greek isles, the chapter samples everything from spicy, heady merguez to loukanika— redolent with fresh oregano and refreshing orange zest.

SPANISH CHORIZO

YIELD: ABOUT 2 POUNDS

A tapas bar staple, Spanish chorizo is distinguished for its use of pimentón, a smoked Spanish paprika. It is not hot but rather distinctively savory. In Spain, you can find this fresh version, ideal for panfrying or grilling, in addition to the ubiquitous cured variety.

EQUIPMENT

Grinder with the coarse (⅜-inch) die
Stuffer
1 metal mixing bowl
Sheet pan
Wire rack

INGREDIENTS

4 feet medium hog casings
2 pounds pork butt, trimmed and cut into
    1-inch cubes
1 tablespoon kosher salt
2 teaspoons freshly ground black pepper
1 tablespoon pimentón or Spanish paprika
    (preferably smoked)
6 garlic cloves, finely chopped
¼ cup red wine

1. Prepare your casings. Refrigerate the mixing bowl and all the grinder and stuffer parts. Freeze the meat, uncovered, for at least 30 minutes.

2. Assemble your grinder. Place the bowl next to the grinder and grind the pork butt into the bowl.

3. Add the salt, pepper, pimentón, garlic, and wine. Knead the mixture for at least 5 minutes.

4. Cook a test piece, taste and adjust the seasonings as preferred, then refrigerate the remaining mix.

5. Assemble your stuffer. Lubricate the horn and slide the casing onto it. Dampen your work surface with water. Stuff the meat into the casing, tying off the open ends at the beginning and end.

6. Prick any air bubbles.

7. Twist off links, alternating directions for each link.

8. Refrigerate overnight, uncovered, on a wire rack set over a sheet pan. Cook or freeze within 3 days.

PROVENÇAL CHICKEN SAUSAGE

YIELD: ABOUT 2 POUNDS

Herbes de Provence is a spice blend that marks much of the cooking of southeast France. Formulations vary, but it typically includes lavender, thyme, savory, and marjoram. Its aromatic yet delicate flavor is an excellent match for chicken.

EQUIPMENT

Grinder with the fine (⅛-inch) die

Stuffer

1 metal mixing bowl

Sheet pan

Wire rack

INGREDIENTS

4 feet medium hog casings

1½ pounds boneless, skinless chicken thighs, cut into 1-inch cubes

½ pound pork back fat, cut into ½-inch cubes

2 teaspoons kosher salt

2 teaspoons freshly ground white pepper

2 tablespoons herbes de Provence

4 garlic cloves, grated

1. Prepare your casings. Refrigerate the mixing bowl and all the grinder and stuffer parts. Freeze the meat and fat, uncovered, for at least 30 minutes.

2. Assemble your grinder. Place the bowl next to the grinder and grind the chicken thighs and pork back fat into the bowl.

3. Add the salt, pepper, herbes de Provence, and garlic. Knead the mixture for at least 5 minutes.

4. Cook a test piece, taste and adjust the seasonings as preferred, then refrigerate the remaining mix.

5. Assemble your stuffer. Lubricate the horn and slide the casing onto it. Dampen your work surface with water. Stuff the meat into the casing, tying off the open ends at the beginning and end.

6. Prick any air bubbles.

7. Twist off links, alternating directions for each link.

8. Refrigerate overnight, uncovered, on a wire rack set over a sheet pan. Cook or freeze within 3 days.

MERGUEZ

YIELD: ABOUT 2¼ POUNDS

Merguez is a North African lamb sausage typically served with couscous. It gets its considerable heat from harissa, a fragrant chili paste made from roasted chiles. It uses a blend of spices including cumin, paprika, and thyme or oregano. Here, we use ras el hanout instead, a traditional spice blend from North Africa. Look for these items in the international specialties aisle of your supermarket.

EQUIPMENT

Grinder with the coarse (⅜-inch) die

Stuffer

1 metal mixing bowl

Sheet pan

Wire rack

INGREDIENTS

6 feet sheep casings

2 pounds boneless lamb shoulder or leg, trimmed and cut into 1-inch cubes

¼ pound pork back fat, cut into ½-inch cubes

2 teaspoons kosher salt

2 teaspoons freshly ground black pepper

6 garlic cloves, grated

2 tablespoons ras el hanout

¼ cup red harissa

1. Prepare your casings. Refrigerate the mixing bowl and all the grinder and stuffer parts. Freeze the meat and fat, uncovered, for at least 30 minutes.

2. Assemble your grinder. Place the bowl next to the grinder and grind the lamb shoulder and pork back fat into the bowl.

3. Add the salt, pepper, garlic, ras el hanout, and harissa. Knead the mixture for at least 5 minutes.

4. Cook a test piece, taste and adjust the seasonings as preferred, then refrigerate the remaining mix.

5. Assemble your stuffer. Lubricate the horn and slide the casing onto it. Dampen your work surface with water. Stuff the meat into the casing, tying off the open ends at the beginning and end.

6. Prick any air bubbles.

7. Twist off links, alternating directions for each link.

8. Refrigerate overnight, uncovered, on a wire rack set over a sheet pan. Cook or freeze within 3 days.

SWEET ITALIAN SAUSAGE

YIELD: ABOUT 2 POUNDS

Paired with sweet peppers and simmered in tomato sauce until soft, sweet Italian sausage is an Italian-American classic. This version is studded with earthy fennel seeds, as well as fresh oregano for an herbaceous accent.

EQUIPMENT

Grinder with the coarse (⅜-inch) die

Stuffer

1 metal mixing bowl

Sheet pan

Wire rack

INGREDIENTS

4 feet medium hog casings

2 pounds pork butt, trimmed and cut into 1-inch cubes

2 teaspoons kosher salt

2 teaspoons freshly ground black pepper

1 tablespoon fennel seeds, toasted if desired

1 tablespoon chopped fresh oregano

6 garlic cloves, grated

1. Prepare your casings. Refrigerate the mixing bowl and all the grinder and stuffer parts. Freeze the meat, uncovered, for at least 30 minutes.

2. Assemble your grinder. Place the bowl next to the grinder and grind the pork butt into the bowl.

3. Add the salt, pepper, fennel seeds, oregano, and garlic. Knead the mixture for at least 5 minutes.

4. Cook a test piece, taste and adjust the seasonings as preferred, then refrigerate the remaining mix.

5. Assemble your stuffer. Lubricate the horn and slide the casing onto it. Dampen your work surface with water. Stuff the meat into the casing, tying off the open ends at the beginning and end.

6. Prick any air bubbles.

7. Twist off links, alternating directions for each link.

8. Refrigerate overnight, uncovered, on a wire rack set over a sheet pan. Cook or freeze within 3 days.

HOT ITALIAN SAUSAGE

YIELD: ABOUT 2 POUNDS

This one is for those who like a burst of heat with their sausage. Crumble this atop pizza to give it an exciting lift, toss it with broccoli rabe and fresh orecchiette for a classic Italian dish, or throw it in your next mixed grill for a worthy addition.

EQUIPMENT

Grinder with the coarse (⅜-inch) die
Stuffer
1 metal mixing bowl
Sheet pan
Wire rack

INGREDIENTS

4 feet medium hog casings
2 pounds pork butt, trimmed and cut into
    1-inch cubes
2 teaspoons kosher salt
2 teaspoons freshly ground black pepper
1 tablespoon fennel seeds, toasted if desired
½ teaspoon cayenne pepper
1 tablespoon chopped fresh oregano
6 garlic cloves, grated

1. Prepare your casings. Refrigerate the mixing bowl and all the grinder and stuffer parts. Freeze the meat, uncovered, for at least 30 minutes.

2. Assemble your grinder. Place the bowl next to the grinder and grind the pork butt into the bowl.

3. Add the salt, pepper, fennel seeds, cayenne, oregano, and garlic. Knead the mixture for at least 5 minutes.

4. Cook a test piece, taste and adjust the seasonings as preferred, then refrigerate the remaining mix.

5. Assemble your stuffer. Lubricate the horn and slide the casing onto it. Dampen your work surface with water. Stuff the meat into the casing, tying off the open ends at the beginning and end.

6. Prick any air bubbles.

7. Twist off links, alternating directions for each link.

8. Refrigerate overnight, uncovered, on a wire rack set over a sheet pan. Cook or freeze within 3 days.

COTECHINO

YIELD: ABOUT 2¼ POUNDS

This sausage is a specialty of Emilia-Romagna, a region known for its hearty cooking. Here, warming spices like cinnamon, cloves, and nutmeg make for an interesting pairing with another one of the region's specialties, Parmigiano-Reggiano cheese.

EQUIPMENT

Grinder with the coarse (⅜-inch) die
Stuffer
1 metal mixing bowl
Sheet pan
Wire rack

INGREDIENTS

4 feet medium hog casings
2 pounds fresh ham with skin, cut into
    1-inch cubes
1 tablespoon kosher salt
2 teaspoons freshly ground black pepper
1 teaspoon allspice
½ teaspoon freshly grated nutmeg
1 teaspoon cinnamon
½ teaspoon toasted ground cloves
½ cup freshly grated Parmigiano-
    Reggiano cheese

1. Prepare your casings. Refrigerate the mixing bowl and all the grinder and stuffer parts. Freeze the meat, uncovered, for at least 30 minutes.

2. Assemble your grinder. Place the bowl next to the grinder and grind the ham into the bowl.

3. Add the salt, pepper, allspice, nutmeg, cinnamon, cloves, and cheese. Knead the mixture for at least 5 minutes.

4. Cook a test piece, taste and adjust the seasonings as preferred, then refrigerate the remaining mix.

5. Assemble your stuffer. Lubricate the horn and slide the casing onto it. Dampen your work surface with water. Stuff the meat into the casing, tying off the open ends at the beginning and end.

6. Prick any air bubbles.

7. Twist off links, alternating directions for each link.

8. Refrigerate overnight, uncovered, on a wire rack set over a sheet pan. Cook or freeze within 3 days.

LUGANEGA

YIELD: ABOUT 2 POUNDS

It is said that this sausage, fragrant with citrus, dates back to Roman times. It's now a specialty of Lombardy, a region in the north of Italy known for risotto. This sausage is typically left in one long coil, which is sold by length.

EQUIPMENT

Grinder with the coarse (⅜-inch) die

Stuffer

1 metal mixing bowl

Sheet pan

Wire rack

INGREDIENTS

4 feet medium hog casings

2 pounds pork butt, trimmed and cut into
    1-inch cubes

1 tablespoon kosher salt

2 teaspoons freshly ground black pepper

½ teaspoon freshly grated nutmeg

2 teaspoons ground toasted coriander seeds

1 teaspoon cinnamon

Zest of 1 lemon

6 garlic cloves, grated

1. Prepare your casings. Refrigerate the mixing bowl and all the grinder and stuffer parts. Freeze the meat, uncovered, for at least 30 minutes.

2. Assemble your grinder. Place the bowl next to the grinder and grind the pork butt into the bowl.

3. Add the salt, pepper, nutmeg, coriander, cinnamon, lemon zest, and garlic. Knead the mixture for at least 5 minutes.

4. Cook a test piece, taste and adjust the seasonings as preferred, then refrigerate the remaining mix.

5. Assemble your stuffer. Lubricate the horn and slide the casing onto it. Dampen your work surface with water. Stuff the meat into the casing, tying off the open ends at the beginning and end.

6. Prick any air bubbles.

7. Refrigerate overnight, uncovered, on a wire rack set over a sheet pan. Cook or freeze within 3 days.

LOUKANIKA

YIELD: ABOUT 2¼ POUNDS

This quintessential Greek sausage is a hearty blend of lamb and pork, seasoned with orange zest and mountainous herbs. Grill or panfry and serve with roasted potatoes, or simmer with a medley of bell peppers.

EQUIPMENT

Grinder with the coarse (⅜-inch) die
Stuffer
1 metal mixing bowl
Sheet pan
Wire rack

INGREDIENTS

4 feet medium hog casings
1 pound pork butt, trimmed and cut into
    1-inch cubes
1 pound boneless lamb shoulder or leg,
    trimmed and cut into 1-inch cubes
¼ pound pork back fat, cut into ½-inch cubes
1 tablespoon kosher salt
2 teaspoons freshly ground black pepper
1 tablespoon finely chopped fresh oregano
2 teaspoons ground toasted coriander seeds
Zest of 1 orange
6 garlic cloves, grated

1. Prepare your casings. Refrigerate the mixing bowl and all the grinder and stuffer parts. Freeze the meat and fat, uncovered, for at least 30 minutes.

2. Assemble your grinder. Place the bowl next to the grinder and grind the pork butt, lamb, and pork back fat into the bowl.

3. Add the salt, pepper, oregano, coriander, orange zest, and garlic. Knead the mixture for at least 5 minutes.

4. Cook a test piece, taste and adjust the seasonings as preferred, then refrigerate the remaining mix.

5. Assemble your stuffer. Lubricate the horn and slide the casing onto it. Dampen your work surface with water. Stuff the meat into the casing, tying off the open ends at the beginning and end.

6. Prick any air bubbles.

7. Twist off links, alternating directions for each link.

8. Refrigerate overnight, uncovered, on a wire rack set over a sheet pan. Cook or freeze within 3 days.

BEYOND THE WEST SAUSAGES

CH. 8

Visit any country where animals are part of the diet, and chances are you'll encounter some kind of sausage. The seasonings, types of meat, and ingredients used to make it are often dictated by what's available locally and by the region's climate. In hot, tropical locales, for example, you're more likely to find chiles and vinegar in the mix, which help sausages keep longer—and of course, make them incredibly delicious. In coastal communities, where land for grazing is precious but seafood is plentiful, you're likely to find sausage made from fish, shrimp, and other types of shellfish. In this chapter, you'll get to sample some truly exciting sausages, which may inspire you to delve deeper into the sausage-making traditions of different cultures.

MEXICAN CHORIZO

YIELD: ABOUT 2 POUNDS

The Mexican version of chorizo is different from the Spanish one. It's hot, vinegary, and crumbly when compared to the European version. It's fantastic for perking up savory breakfast dishes, tacos, and chili. If you can find it, Mexican dried oregano imparts an even more authentic flavor to this sausage.

EQUIPMENT

Grinder with the coarse (⅜-inch) die
Stuffer
1 metal mixing bowl
Sheet pan
Wire rack

INGREDIENTS

4 feet medium hog casings
2 pounds pork butt, trimmed and cut into
    1-inch cubes
1 tablespoon kosher salt
2 teaspoons freshly ground black pepper
1 teaspoon cayenne pepper
2 teaspoons paprika
2 teaspoons ground toasted cumin seeds
2 teaspoons ground toasted coriander seeds
2 teaspoons dried oregano
6 garlic cloves, finely chopped
1 jalapeño, stemmed, seeded, and finely diced
¼ cup white vinegar

1. Prepare your casings. Refrigerate the mixing bowl and all the grinder and stuffer parts. Freeze the meat, uncovered, for at least 30 minutes.

2. Assemble your grinder. Place the bowl next to the grinder and grind the pork butt into the bowl.

3. Add the salt, pepper, cayenne, paprika, cumin, coriander, oregano, garlic, jalapeño, and vinegar. Knead the mixture for at least 5 minutes.

4. Cook a test piece, taste and adjust the seasonings as preferred, then refrigerate the remaining mix.

5. Assemble your stuffer. Lubricate the horn and slide the casing onto it. Dampen your work surface with water. Stuff the meat into the casing, tying off the open ends at the beginning and end.

6. Prick any air bubbles.

7. Twist off links, alternating directions for each link.

8. Refrigerate overnight, uncovered, on a wire rack set over a sheet pan. Cook or freeze within 3 days.

ĆEVAPI

YIELD: ABOUT 2¼ POUNDS

These skinless, finger-length sausages are beloved throughout the Balkan region, and are typically grilled over charcoal. They can be made from beef, lamb, pork, or a combination of the three. Here, baking powder helps achieve an almost bouncy texture.

EQUIPMENT

Grinder with the coarse (⅜-inch) die
Stuffer
1 metal mixing bowl
Sheet pan
Wire rack

INGREDIENTS

4 feet medium hog casings
1 pound pork butt, trimmed and cut into
    1-inch cubes
1 pound boneless lamb shoulder or leg,
    trimmed and cut into 1-inch cubes
¼ pound pork back fat, cut into ½-inch cubes
1 tablespoon kosher salt
2 teaspoons freshly ground black pepper
2 teaspoons paprika
1 tablespoon baking powder
6 garlic cloves, grated

1. Prepare your casings. Refrigerate the mixing bowl and all the grinder and stuffer parts. Freeze the meat and fat, uncovered, for at least 30 minutes.

2. Assemble your grinder. Place the bowl next to the grinder and grind the pork butt, lamb, and pork back fat into the bowl.

3. Add the salt, pepper, paprika, baking powder, and garlic. Knead the mixture for at least 5 minutes.

4. Cook a test piece, taste and adjust the seasonings as preferred, then refrigerate the remaining mix.

5. Take 1½ to 2 ounces of the mixture at a time and roll it between your hands to form into logs.

6. Refrigerate the logs overnight, covered, on a wire rack set over a sheet pan. Cook or freeze within 3 days.

OTAK-OTAK

YIELD: ABOUT 2 POUNDS

Translated literally, the name of this Indonesian fish sausage means "brain-brain," perhaps a reference to its appearance. It is traditionally wrapped in banana leaves, then grilled or steamed. We use sheep casings instead here—a bit easier to find and perfectly suitable for the task.

EQUIPMENT

Grinder with the fine (⅛-inch) die
Stuffer
1 metal mixing bowl
Sheet pan
Wire rack

INGREDIENTS

6 feet sheep casings
2 pounds whitefish fillets, such as tilapia, trimmed and cut into 1-inch cubes
1 teaspoon kosher salt
1 teaspoon freshly ground white pepper
2 tablespoons cornstarch
¼ cup full-fat coconut milk
1 tablespoon sugar
¼ cup thinly sliced scallions, white and green parts

1. Prepare your casings. Refrigerate the mixing bowl and all the grinder and stuffer parts. Freeze the fish, uncovered, for at least 30 minutes.

2. Assemble your grinder. Place the bowl next to the grinder and grind the whitefish fillets into the bowl.

3. Add the salt, pepper, cornstarch, coconut milk (shake the can vigorously before opening), sugar, and scallions. Knead the mixture for at least 5 minutes.

4. Cook a test piece, taste and adjust the seasonings as preferred, then refrigerate the remaining mix.

5. Assemble your stuffer. Lubricate the horn and slide the casing onto it. Dampen your work surface with water. Stuff the fish into the casing, tying off the open ends at the beginning and end.

6. Prick any air bubbles.

7. Twist off links, alternating directions for each link.

8. Refrigerate overnight, uncovered, on a wire rack set over a sheet pan. Cook or freeze within 3 days.

VIETNAMESE SHRIMP SAUSAGE (CHAO TOM)

YIELD: ABOUT 2¼ POUNDS

This Vietnamese sausage is traditionally served wrapped around a piece of sugarcane. We use hog casings here, but you can also roll a couple of ounces of the mixture between your hands to form logs.

EQUIPMENT

Grinder with the fine (⅛-inch) die

Stuffer

1 metal mixing bowl

Sheet pan

Wire rack

INGREDIENTS

4 feet medium hog casings

2 pounds shrimp, peeled and deveined

¼ pound pork back fat, cut into ½-inch cubes

1 teaspoon fish sauce

1 teaspoon freshly ground white pepper

2 tablespoons sugar

2 teaspoons baking powder

6 garlic cloves, grated

1. Prepare your casings. Refrigerate the mixing bowl and all the grinder and stuffer parts. Freeze the shrimp and fat, uncovered, for at least 30 minutes.

2. Assemble your grinder. Place the bowl next to the grinder and grind the shrimp and pork back fat into the bowl.

3. Add the fish sauce, pepper, sugar, baking powder, and garlic. Knead the mixture for at least 5 minutes.

4. Cook a test piece, taste and adjust the vseasonings as preferred, then refrigerate the remaining mix.

5. Assemble your stuffer. Lubricate the horn and slide the casing onto it. Dampen your work surface with water. Stuff the meat into the casing, tying off the open ends at the beginning and end.

6. Prick any air bubbles.

7. Twist off links, alternating directions for each link.

8. Refrigerate overnight, uncovered, on a wire rack set over a sheet pan. Cook or freeze within 3 days.

FILIPINO LONGANISA

YIELD: ABOUT 2 POUNDS

The Spanish brought their sausage-making traditions with them when they came to the Philippines in the late 16th century. This sausage is the Filipino version of longaniza, a Spanish sausage. The addition of vinegar gives it a distinct tang.

EQUIPMENT

Grinder with the coarse (⅜-inch) die
Stuffer
1 metal mixing bowl
Sheet pan
Wire rack

INGREDIENTS

4 feet medium hog casings
2 pounds pork butt, trimmed and cut into
    1-inch cubes
1 tablespoon kosher salt
2 teaspoons freshly ground black pepper
½ teaspoon cayenne pepper
2 teaspoons paprika
2 teaspoons dried oregano
6 garlic cloves, finely chopped
¼ cup white vinegar

1. Prepare your casings. Refrigerate the mixing bowl and all the grinder and stuffer parts. Freeze the meat, uncovered, for at least 30 minutes.

2. Assemble your grinder. Place the bowl next to the grinder and grind the pork butt into the bowl.

3. Add the salt, pepper, cayenne, paprika, oregano, garlic, and vinegar. Knead the mixture for at least 5 minutes.

4. Cook a test piece, taste and adjust the seasonings as preferred, then refrigerate the remaining mix.

5. Assemble your stuffer. Lubricate the horn and slide the casing onto it. Dampen your work surface with water. Stuff the meat into the casing, tying off the open ends at the beginning and end.

6. Prick any air bubbles.

7. Twist off links, alternating directions for each link.

8. Refrigerate overnight, uncovered, on a wire rack set over a sheet pan. Cook or freeze within 3 days.

VIETNAMESE CHICKEN SAUSAGE

YIELD: ABOUT 2 POUNDS

The flavors in this sausage are inspired by bánh mì, a Vietnamese sandwich that features grilled meats in a buttered baguette, brightened with cilantro and spiced up with jalapeño.

EQUIPMENT

Grinder with the fine (⅛-inch) die
Stuffer
1 metal mixing bowl
Sheet pan
Wire rack

INGREDIENTS

4 feet medium hog casings
1½ pounds boneless, skinless chicken thighs, cut into 1-inch cubes
½ pound pork back fat, cut into ½-inch cubes
2 tablespoons fish sauce
2 teaspoons freshly ground white pepper
1 jalapeño, stemmed, seeded, and finely diced
2 tablespoons minced lemongrass
2 tablespoons finely chopped fresh cilantro
¼ cup rice vinegar
2 tablespoons sugar

1. Prepare your casings. Refrigerate the mixing bowl and all the grinder and stuffer parts. Freeze the meat and fat, uncovered, for at least 30 minutes.

2. Assemble your grinder. Place the bowl next to the grinder and grind the chicken thighs and pork back fat into the bowl.

3. Add the fish sauce, pepper, jalapeño, lemongrass, cilantro, rice vinegar, and sugar. Knead the mixture for at least 5 minutes.

4. Cook a test piece, taste and adjust the seasonings as preferred, then refrigerate the remaining mix.

5. Assemble your stuffer. Lubricate the horn and slide the casing onto it. Dampen your work surface with water. Stuff the meat into the casing, tying off the open ends at the beginning and end.

6. Prick any air bubbles.

7. Twist off links, alternating directions for each link.

8. Refrigerate overnight, uncovered, on a wire rack set over a sheet pan. Cook or freeze within 3 days.

PART 3

COOKING WITH SAUSAGE

BREAKFAST

CH. 9

Breakfast is the most important meal of the day, no matter when you decide to have it, and what better way to perk it up than by adding some delicious sausage to your daily routine? In this chapter, you'll find make-ahead recipes that are perfect for breakfast on the go, breakfast dishes fit for dinner, and breakfast favorites for a leisurely Sunday morning. Start the day off with Spicy Breakfast Burritos featuring Southwestern Sausage (page 48). Treat yourself to a glass of bubbly and some Garlic Sausage Veggie Frittata at the end of a long, hard day. Or jump-start your morning with a stack of Maple-Bacon Sausage Pancakes. And if you've truly got a sweet tooth, don't miss out on the Sausage Monkey Bread— you'll go absolutely bananas for it.

SPICY BREAKFAST SAUSAGE BAKE

SERVES 6 | PREP TIME: 10 MINUTES | COOK TIME: 1 HOUR 10 MINUTES

There's nothing better than sausage for breakfast, especially when combined with other hearty ingredients. This sweet-and-spicy recipe will wake up your taste buds. The combination of hash browns and homemade sausage flavored with bacon is absolutely delicious and will fuel you up for the rest of the day. I suggest serving this with coffee, orange juice, and fresh fruit such as grapefruit or mixed berries.

Nonstick cooking spray

2 tablespoons (¼-stick) butter

1 pound Maple-Bacon Breakfast Sausage (page 44)

1 onion, chopped

2 garlic cloves, minced

1 jalapeño pepper, minced

1 (20-ounce) package frozen hash-brown potatoes, thawed and drained

2 cups shredded Swiss cheese

6 eggs

⅓ cup light cream

½ teaspoon salt

⅛ teaspoon cayenne pepper

¼ cup grated Parmesan cheese

1. Preheat the oven to 375°F. Spray a 9-by-13-inch glass baking dish with nonstick cooking spray and set aside.

2. Melt the butter in a large skillet over medium heat. Add the sausages and cook, turning occasionally with tongs, for 5 to 8 minutes, or until they are cooked and golden brown.

3. Remove the sausages from the skillet and drain on paper towels. Cut each sausage in half crosswise.

4. Add the onion, garlic, and jalapeño to the drippings remaining in the skillet and cook over medium heat, stirring frequently, for 4 to 6 minutes, or until tender.

5. Combine the cooked-onion mixture with the hash-brown potatoes and Swiss cheese in the prepared dish. Top with the cooked sausages, nestling them into the potato mixture.

6. In a medium bowl, combine the eggs, cream, salt, and cayenne and beat well with a wire whisk. Pour this mixture over the ingredients in the dish.

7. Top with the Parmesan cheese.

8. Bake for 45 to 55 minutes, or until the casserole is browned and puffed up. Cut into squares to serve.

SCRAMBLED EGGS WITH CHICKEN SAUSAGE

SERVES 6 | PREP TIME: 10 MINUTES | COOK TIME: 25 MINUTES

Scrambled eggs may seem like a boring breakfast dish that everyone makes, but this recipe is anything but ordinary. A chicken sausage flavored with herbs from France peps up this morning staple, and colorful and tasty veggies such as bell peppers and summer squash add flavor and nutrition. To make the best scrambled eggs, be sure to beat the egg mixture well before you cook it. And stir the eggs only occasionally as they cook, so they form big, fluffy curds.

3 tablespoons butter

1 pound Provençal Chicken
    Sausage (page 75)

1 green bell pepper, chopped

1 yellow summer squash, chopped

2 garlic cloves, minced

12 eggs

⅓ cup light cream

1 teaspoon salt

1 teaspoon dried thyme

⅛ teaspoon freshly ground black pepper

1. In a large skillet, melt the butter over medium heat.

2. Add the sausages and cook, turning occasionally with tongs, until they are cooked through and browned.

3. Remove the sausages to a paper towel to drain. Cut into ½-inch pieces.

4. Add the bell pepper, squash, and garlic to the drippings remaining in the skillet. Cook over medium heat for 4 to 6 minutes, stirring occasionally, until tender.

5. Meanwhile, beat the eggs, cream, salt, thyme, and pepper in a large bowl.

6. When the vegetables are tender, add the egg mixture to the skillet.

7. Cook over medium-low heat, stirring occasionally, until the eggs are set but still moist.

8. Stir the sausages into the egg mixture.

9. Serve immediately.

GARLIC SAUSAGE VEGGIE FRITTATA

SERVES 6 | PREP TIME: 15 MINUTES | COOK TIME: 50 MINUTES

A frittata is like an omelet, but not as fragile. This dish comes from Italy, and frittata translates to "fried." In a frittata, additional ingredients are mixed in with the eggs, instead of filling the egg mixture, as happens in an omelet. This egg dish can be served hot or warm, or even at room temperature. It's sturdy and can be flavored in many different ways. (You'll need an ovenproof skillet for this recipe.)

2 tablespoons olive oil

1 pound Garlic Sausage (page 57)

1 onion, finely chopped

2 garlic cloves, minced

1 red bell pepper, chopped

1 cup button mushrooms, sliced

12 eggs

¼ cup whole milk

1 teaspoon salt

1 teaspoon dried basil

1½ cups shredded provolone cheese

3 tablespoons grated Romano cheese

1. Preheat the oven to 350°F.

2. In a 10-inch ovenproof skillet, heat the olive oil over medium heat.

3. Add the sausages and cook, turning occasionally with tongs, until they are cooked through and browned.

4. Remove the sausages from the pan and drain on paper towels. Cut the sausages into 1-inch pieces.

5. Add the onion, garlic, bell pepper, and mushrooms to the drippings remaining in the skillet. Cook over medium heat, stirring occasionally, until tender, about 5 to 8 minutes.

6. Meanwhile, beat the eggs with the milk, salt, and basil in a large bowl.

7. When the vegetables are tender, return the sausage pieces to the skillet.

8. Pour half of the eggs over the mixture in the skillet and sprinkle with half of the provolone cheese.

9. Top with the remaining eggs and remaining provolone cheese. Sprinkle with the Romano cheese.

10. Bake the frittata in the oven for 25 to 35 minutes, or until set and light golden brown.

11. Cut into wedges to serve.

SAUSAGE, ARTICHOKE, AND PEPPER OMELET

SERVES 4 | PREP TIME: 15 MINUTES | COOK TIME: 15 MINUTES

Sausages add great flavor and character to an ordinary breakfast omelet. You can use any sausage you'd like in this recipe, but Provençal Chicken Sausage with its flavors of France is perfect for a morning meal. Artichoke hearts add another touch of France, and are slightly exotic. You can find them in cans or the frozen aisle at your grocery store. I suggest serving this recipe with coffee, orange juice, and buttered whole-wheat toast.

2 tablespoons (¼-stick) butter

1 pound Provençal Chicken Sausage (page 75)

½ cup minced onion

2 garlic cloves, minced

1 red bell pepper, chopped

1 (10-ounce) can artichoke hearts, drained and chopped

9 eggs

2 tablespoons light cream

½ teaspoon salt

⅛ teaspoon freshly ground black pepper

1 teaspoon dried thyme

1½ cups shredded Gruyère cheese

1. In a 10-inch nonstick skillet, melt the butter over medium heat.

2. Add the sausages and cook, turning occasionally with tongs, until they are cooked through and browned.

3. Remove the sausages from the skillet and drain on paper towels. Cut the sausages into ½-inch pieces and set aside.

4. Add the onion, garlic, and bell pepper to the drippings in the skillet. Sauté for 3 to 4 minutes, stirring frequently, until tender.

5. Remove the vegetables from the skillet with a slotted spoon. Combine with the sausages and the artichoke hearts in a medium bowl.

6. Beat the eggs with the cream, salt, pepper, and thyme in a large bowl.

7. Pour the egg mixture into the skillet. Cook over medium heat, shaking the pan occasionally, until the eggs are set, but still moist and lightly browned underneath. (Run a spatula under the eggs occasionally to loosen.)

8. Top the eggs with the sausage mixture and the cheese.

9. Using a spatula, carefully fold the omelet to enclose the filling.

10. Cover the pan and cook, shaking the pan occasionally, for another 1 to 2 minutes to melt the cheese.

11. Cut into wedges and serve immediately.

MINI BAKED SAUSAGE FRITTATAS

MAKES 12 FRITTATAS | PREP TIME: 15 MINUTES | COOK TIME: 35 MINUTES

Mini frittatas are baked in muffin cups, and they are wonderful for breakfast on the go. These little frittatas are sturdy enough to eat out of your hand. They are filled with cheese, flavorful Beef Breakfast Sausage, green onion, and mushrooms. You can make these little frittatas ahead of time, cool them for about 30 minutes at room temperature, and then refrigerate. Eat them cold out of the refrigerator or rewarm in the microwave oven.

Nonstick cooking spray

1 tablespoon (⅛-stick) butter

1 tablespoon olive oil

½ pound Beef Breakfast Sausage (page 43)

⅓ cup chopped green onion

1 cup chopped cremini mushrooms

7 eggs

½ cup milk

½ teaspoon salt

⅛ teaspoon freshly ground black pepper

1 cup shredded Colby cheese

1. Preheat the oven to 375°F. Spray a 12-cup muffin tin with nonstick cooking spray and set aside.

2. Heat the butter and olive oil in a large skillet over medium heat.

3. Remove the sausages from the casings and crumble it into the skillet.

4. Cook and stir the sausage until it is browned and fully cooked, about 8 to 10 minutes.

5. Add the green onion and mushrooms to the skillet. Cook, stirring occasionally, for 4 to 5 minutes more, until tender.

6. Beat the eggs, milk, salt, and pepper in a large bowl.

7. Stir in the sausage mixture and the Colby cheese.

8. Divide the mixture among the prepared muffin cups, putting about ¼ cup of the egg mixture into each cup.

9. Bake for 14 to 19 minutes, or until the mini frittatas are set and lightly browned on top.

10. Serve immediately, or remove the frittatas from the muffin cups and cool for 30 minutes, then refrigerate until cold.

SAUSAGE AND PEAR STRATA

SERVES 6 | PREP TIME: 15 MINUTES, PLUS 8 HOURS TO CHILL | COOK TIME: 1 HOUR

A strata is made by combining cubes of bread with a custard mixture and other ingredients, and then baking until the strata is puffy and golden brown. You can use any type of bread in this recipe, but a cracked-wheat bread will add texture and interest to the dish. The best pears to use in this recipe are Bosc or Anjou. The pears should be firm but yield slightly to pressure. This recipe must be made the night before you want to eat it.

Nonstick cooking spray
2 tablespoons (¼-stick) butter
1 pound Pork Breakfast Sausage (page 42)
4 Bosc or Anjou pears, cored and chopped
2 tablespoons honey
10 eggs
2½ cups milk
½ teaspoon salt
¼ teaspoon freshly grated nutmeg
10 slices cracked-wheat or whole-wheat
    bread, cubed
½ cup dried cranberries

1. Spray a 9-by-13-inch glass baking dish with nonstick cooking spray and set aside.

2. Melt the butter in a large skillet over medium heat.

3. Add the sausages and cook, turning occasionally with tongs, until they are cooked through and browned.

4. Remove the sausages from the skillet and drain on paper towels. Cut into 1-inch pieces.

5. Add the pears to the drippings in the skillet and drizzle with honey. Cook, stirring frequently, over medium heat until the pears are softened, about 3 minutes.

6. Beat the eggs in a large bowl with the milk, salt, and nutmeg.

7. Layer the bread, cranberries, cooked pears, and sausages in the prepared baking dish.

8. Pour the egg mixture over the bread mixture in the dish.

9. Cover the dish and refrigerate for at least 8 hours, or overnight.

10. When you're ready to eat, preheat the oven to 350°F.

11. Uncover the strata. Bake for 45 to 55 minutes, or until the strata is puffed, golden brown, and cooked through.

12. Cut into squares to serve.

APPLE SAUSAGE WAFFLE BAKE

SERVES 8 | PREP TIME: 15 MINUTES, PLUS 8 HOURS TO CHILL | COOK TIME: 1 HOUR 10 MINUTES

Most stratas and other breakfast bakes using bread products in custard are made with cubes of bread. This recipe starts with waffles for a great texture and flavor contrast. Frozen toaster waffles are perfectly appropriate for this recipe, but you can use homemade waffles if you'd like. Apples add a wonderful touch of sweetness, and the sage complements the flavors of the dish perfectly. Prepare this dish the night before you want to serve it, then bake it in the morning.

Nonstick cooking spray

1 tablespoon olive oil

1 pound Apple–Sage Chicken
    Sausage (page 45)

4 Granny Smith or Cortland apples,
    cored and chopped

8 frozen waffles, toasted, cooled, and cubed

7 eggs

1½ cups whole milk

½ cup apple juice

1 teaspoon salt

½ teaspoon dried sage

⅛ teaspoon freshly ground black pepper

1 cup shredded Havarti cheese

1. Spray a 9-by-13-inch glass baking dish with nonstick cooking spray and set aside.

2. In a large skillet, heat the olive oil over medium heat. Add the sausages and cook, turning occasionally with tongs, until cooked through and golden brown.

3. Drain the sausages on paper towels and cut into 2-inch pieces.

4. Add the apples to the drippings in the skillet. Cook over medium heat, stirring occasionally, until the apples are tender, about 7 to 9 minutes.

5. Layer the waffle cubes, sausage pieces, and apples in the prepared baking dish.

6. In a large bowl, combine the eggs, milk, apple juice, salt, sage, and pepper, and beat with a whisk until combined.

7. Pour the eggs mixture over the ingredients in the dish and sprinkle with the Havarti cheese.

8. Cover the dish and refrigerate for at least 8 hours, or overnight.

9. In the morning, preheat the oven to 375°F.

10. Uncover the strata and bake for 40 to 50 minutes, or until the casserole is puffed and light golden brown.

11. Cut into squares to serve.

MAPLE-BACON SAUSAGE PANCAKES

SERVES 4 | PREP TIME: 15 MINUTES | COOK TIME: 15 MINUTES

Everyone loves pancakes. But did you know you can have pancakes and sausages all in one bite? Adding cooked sausages to pancake batter is a great way to add flavor and interest to this classic breakfast dish. The sausage makes the pancakes taste slightly smoked, a perfect foil for sweet syrup. Serve these pancakes with warm maple syrup or honey, along with fresh fruit such as grapefruit, oranges, or clementines.

1 pound Maple-Bacon Breakfast
    Sausage (page 44)
2 tablespoons butter (¼-stick), plus
    4 tablespoons (½-stick)
1¼ cups all-purpose flour
¾ cup whole-wheat flour
¼ cup brown sugar
2 teaspoons baking powder
½ teaspoon baking soda
½ teaspoon salt
2 eggs
2 cups buttermilk

1. Remove the sausages from the casings. Crumble into a skillet and add 2 tablespoons of butter.

2. Cook the sausage over medium heat, stirring to break it up, until it is cooked through and browned. Set aside.

3. In a large bowl, combine the all-purpose flour, whole-wheat flour, brown sugar, baking powder, baking soda, and salt. Mix well.

4. Add the eggs and buttermilk to the bowl. Mix just until the ingredients are combined. Do not overbeat, or the pancakes will be tough.

5. Fold in the cooked-sausage mixture along with the drippings.

6. Melt the remaining 4 tablespoons of butter in a large nonstick skillet over medium heat.

7. Add the pancake batter, ¼ cup at a time, to the skillet.

8. Cook the pancakes until bubbles form on the surface and start to break, and the pancakes look crisp around the edges.

9. Carefully turn the pancakes using a spatula and cook for another 2 minutes on the other side.

10. Serve immediately with warm maple syrup.

BREAKFAST SAUSAGE CROISSANTS

SERVES 8 | PREP TIME: 15 MINUTES | COOK TIME: 25 MINUTES

The breakfast sandwiches you get from fast-food restaurants are good, but nothing compares to homemade breakfast sandwiches. Your own home-made sausage is the secret ingredient of this recipe. These Breakfast Sausage Croissants are made with real puff pastry, so they are very flaky and flavorful. A perfect breakfast recipe to eat as you are running out the door to start your day.

2 tablespoons (¼-stick) butter

1 pound Honey Mustard Chicken Sausage (page 47)

1 (17-ounce) package frozen puff pastry, thawed

3 tablespoons Dijon mustard

½ cup soft garlic-and-herb spreadable cheese

1 egg, beaten

1. Preheat the oven to 375°F. Line a cookie sheet with parchment paper and set aside.

2. Melt the butter in a large saucepan over medium heat. Add the sausages and cook, turning occasionally with tongs, until they are cooked through and browned.

3. Remove the sausages from the skillet and place on paper towels. Let them cool while you prepare the rest of the recipe.

4. Unroll the puff pastry and place each sheet on a lightly floured surface.

5. Cut each sheet into 4 equal squares. Cut each of the squares into 2 triangles, making 16 triangles in all.

6. Spread each piece of pastry with mustard, then add the spreadable cheese.

7. Place one sausage on each triangle at the wide end.

8. Roll up the pastries, enclosing the sausages. Seal the edges.

9. Place the sausage-filled pastries on the prepared cookie sheet and brush each with some of the beaten egg.

10. Bake for 15 to 20 minutes, or until the pastry is puffed and golden brown.

SPICY BREAKFAST BURRITOS

MAKES 24 BURRITOS | PREP TIME: 15 MINUTES | COOK TIME: 15 MINUTES

Burritos for breakfast? Why not? This spicy and tasty recipe is perfect to make ahead of time because you can freeze the individual burritos. Then, when you want a quick breakfast, grab one out of the freezer, microwave it for a few minutes, and you have a hearty and warming meal ready in no time. And if you cannot wait, go ahead and eat these burritos right away.

1 pound Southwestern Sausage (page 48)

1 tablespoon olive oil

1 onion, chopped

3 garlic cloves, minced

1 jalapeño pepper, minced

14 eggs

¼ cup light cream

1 teaspoon salt

⅛ teaspoon freshly ground black pepper

1 teaspoon chili powder

⅔ cup tomato salsa

2 cups shredded pepper Jack cheese

24 (10- to 12-inch) flour tortillas

1.   In a large skillet, cook the sausages over medium heat, turning occasionally with tongs, until they are cooked through and browned.

2.   Remove the sausages from the skillet and place on paper towels to drain. Cut into ½-inch pieces.

3.   Add the olive oil to the drippings in the skillet. Add the onion, garlic, and jalapeño. Cook over medium heat, stirring occasionally, for 4 to 6 minutes or until tender.

4.   Remove the vegetables from the skillet with a slotted spoon and put in a bowl with the sausages.

5.   In a medium bowl, beat the eggs with the cream, salt, pepper, and chili powder. Pour the mixture into the skillet with the drippings.

6. Cook the eggs over medium heat, stirring occasionally, until they are set but still moist.

7. Assemble the burritos. Divide the egg mixture, sausage mixture, salsa, and cheese equally among the tortillas and roll them up.

8. You can eat the burritos immediately. If you want to eat at a later time, fasten them closed with a toothpick, wrap in foil or plastic wrap, and freeze.

9. To reheat, unwrap a burrito and remove the toothpick. Microwave on high for 1 to 2 minutes, or until hot. You can also bake the frozen burritos at 375°F for 10 to 15 minutes or until hot.

ROSEMARY-LAMB SAUSAGE AND VEGGIE QUICHE

SERVES 4 | PREP TIME: 15 MINUTES | COOK TIME: 1 HOUR 5 MINUTES

Eating quiche for breakfast or brunch is very luxurious; it doesn't feel right to me unless I'm sitting down with a fancy table setting and fresh flowers. This recipe looks complicated, but it's really very easy. Perfect for a leisurely weekend meal. If you can't find fresh rosemary, don't use dried; the little needles will be too hard and sharp in the dish. Serve this quiche with fresh strawberries and blueberries for a great meal.

1 (9-inch) pastry shell

½ pound Rosemary-Lamb Sausage (page 46)

2 tablespoons butter (¼ stick)

1 onion, chopped

1 cup chopped leeks

2 garlic cloves, minced

4 eggs

1¼ cups light cream

½ cup sour cream

1 teaspoon salt

2 teaspoons chopped fresh rosemary

¼ teaspoon freshly ground black pepper

1⅓ cups shredded Gruyère or Swiss cheese

2 tablespoons grated Parmesan cheese

1. Preheat the oven to 400°F. Prepare the pastry dough if you're making it yourself. If you are using a premade, refrigerated pastry shell, put it into a 9-inch pan, flute the edges, and set aside.

2. In a large skillet, add the sausages and cook over medium heat, turning occasionally with tongs, until they are cooked through and browned.

3. Remove the sausages from the skillet and place on paper towels to drain. Cut into 1-inch pieces, and set aside.

4. Add the butter to the drippings remaining in the skillet, then add the onion, leeks, and garlic. Cook, stirring occasionally, until the vegetables are tender, about 5 to 8 minutes.

5. Beat the eggs, light cream, sour cream, salt, rosemary, and pepper in a medium bowl.

6. Put half of the sausages and half of the vegetables into the pie shell. Sprinkle with half of the Gruyère cheese. Repeat to create another layer.

7. Pour the egg mixture into the pie shell. Shake the shell gently so the egg mixture goes all the way to the bottom.

8. Sprinkle the pie with the Parmesan cheese.

9. Bake for 45 to 55 minutes, or until the quiche is puffed, set, and golden brown. Cut into wedges to serve.

SAUSAGE MONKEY BREAD

SERVES 12 | PREP TIME: 20 MINUTES, PLUS 1 HOUR TO LET RISE | COOK TIME: 45 MINUTES

Monkey bread is named, apparently, because you pull off individual pieces of bread from a loaf, just like . . . monkeys? I guess so! At any rate, this bread is fun to make and eat, and it's a great choice if you're feeding a crowd. Most of these recipes use refrigerated biscuits for the "bread" part of the recipe. But bread dough is a better choice. It is more tender and flavorful. Yum!

Nonstick cooking spray

1 pound Maple-Bacon Breakfast
    Sausage (page 44)

½ cup butter (1 stick), melted

½ cup brown sugar

¼ cup maple syrup

2 (16-ounce) loaves frozen bread
    dough, thawed

⅔ cup granulated sugar

2 tablespoons flour

1 teaspoon cinnamon

1. Spray a 12-inch Bundt pan with nonstick baking spray containing flour, and set aside.

2. Add the sausages to a large skillet and cook over medium heat, turning occasionally with tongs, until cooked through and browned. Remove the sausages from the skillet and place on paper towels to drain. Cut the sausages into 1-inch pieces and set aside.

3. In a medium saucepan, combine the butter, brown sugar, and maple syrup over low heat. Cook, stirring continuously, until the mixture combines. Remove the pan from the heat.

4. Divide each loaf of dough into 4 pieces, then divide those into 6 balls, making 24 balls for each loaf, or 48 balls in total.

5. Wrap each ball of dough around a piece of sausage. If you don't have enough sausage for the dough balls, that's fine—biting into one will be a surprise!

6. Put the sugar, flour, and cinnamon on a large plate. Mix gently to combine. Roll the filled dough balls in the sugar mixture to coat.

7. Pour ¼ of the butter mixture into the prepared Bundt pan.

8. Top with half of the dough balls, arranging them in the pan. You don't have to be precise with the layering.

9. Drizzle half of the remaining butter mixture over the dough.

10. Repeat with the remaining dough balls and remaining butter mixture.

11. Cover and let rise for about 1 hour at room temperature.

12. Preheat the oven to 350°F. Bake the bread for 30 to 40 minutes or until it is golden brown.

13. Remove the bread from the oven. Using oven mitts to protect your hands, invert the pan over a serving plate—be careful, the sugar syrup is hot.

14. Let the bread cool for 10 minutes, then enjoy.

SOUPS & STEWS

CH. 10

Few things get you through a chilly winter night quite like a hearty soup, stew, or chowder, and the addition of sausage can transform a good bowl into something great. In this chapter, you'll find sausage paired with traditional flavors, as well as more creative concoctions. Fresh kielbasa, typically used in Polish cooking to make rich soups, is simmered along with bright, herbaceous dill in Fresh Kielbasa and Sauerkraut Soup. Heartwarming Beef Chili Con Carne Sausage (page 53) brings Tex-Mex flavor to Crockpot Sausage and Black Bean Chili—for a meal that will become a favorite. And for something that'll stick to your ribs, try the Creole Soup featuring Chaurice (page 50), inspired by the dynamic cooking of New Orleans.

FRESH KIELBASA AND SAUERKRAUT SOUP

SERVES 6 | PREP TIME: 15 MINUTES | COOK TIME: 50 MINUTES

Sausage and sauerkraut go together like peanut butter and jelly or ham and cheese. You can find sauerkraut in the canned-vegetable aisle of the supermarket, or I've occasionally found fresh varieties in the refrigerated section near the hot dogs. This salty, fermented mixture of cabbage and spices is perfect with smoky sausage. Mushrooms, onions, and carrots round out the vegetables in this flavorful soup. Serve it with a ranch salad tossed with avocados and a tall glass of beer.

2 tablespoons olive oil

1 pound Fresh Kielbasa (page 56)

1 onion, chopped

3 garlic cloves, minced

1 (8-ounce) package cremini
    mushrooms, sliced

1 (16-ounce) package baby carrots

1 (16-ounce) can sauerkraut, drained

5 cups chicken stock

1 tablespoon chopped fresh dill weed

1 teaspoon honey

1. In a large soup pot or Dutch oven, heat the olive oil over medium heat.

2. Add the sausages and cook, turning occasionally with tongs, until they are cooked and browned.

3. Remove the sausages from the pot and cut into 1-inch slices.

4. Add the onion, garlic, and mushrooms to the drippings in the pot. Cook, stirring occasionally, until crisp-tender, about 5 minutes.

5. Return the sausage pieces to the skillet. Add the carrots, sauerkraut, chicken stock, dill, and honey.

6. Bring the soup to a simmer.

7. Partially cover the pot and continue to simmer for 30 to 40 minutes, or until the vegetables are tender, and serve.

SAUSAGE CORN AND POTATO CHOWDER

SERVES 6 TO 8 | PREP TIME: 15 MINUTES | COOK TIME: 1 HOUR 5 MINUTES

A chowder is a thick soup that is made with cream and often cheese. Chowders usually include potatoes and lots of vegetables. This classic recipe is true comfort food, wonderful on a cold winter night when sleet is ticking against your windows. Serve this delicious chowder with any type of cracker or toasted garlic bread, a simple green salad drizzled with a vinaigrette, and rosé wine.

1 pound Bratwurst (page 59)

2 tablespoons olive oil

2 onions, chopped

5 garlic cloves, minced

1 (8-ounce) package button
    mushrooms, sliced

4 large carrots, peeled and sliced

3 russet potatoes, peeled and cubed

1 (16-ounce) package frozen corn

5 cups chicken stock

1 teaspoon dried marjoram

1 teaspoon salt

⅛ teaspoon freshly ground black pepper

1½ cups light cream

3 tablespoons cornstarch

1½ cups shredded Swiss cheese

1. In a large soup pot or Dutch oven, cook the sausages over medium heat, turning occasionally with tongs, until cooked through and browned.

2. Remove the sausages from the pot and cut into 1-inch pieces. Set aside.

3. Add the olive oil to the pot.

4. Add the onions, garlic, and mushrooms to the pot. Cook, stirring, over medium heat until crisp-tender, about 5 minutes.

5. Add the carrots, potatoes, corn, and sausages to the pot and pour the chicken stock over the mixture. Add the marjoram, salt, and pepper.

6. Partially cover the pot and simmer for 40 to 50 minutes, or until the vegetables are tender.

continued

7. Combine the cream and cornstarch in a small bowl and mix well. Add to the soup.

8. Cook and stir over low heat until the soup starts to thicken.

9. Stir in the Swiss cheese and cook until melted, then serve.

CROCKPOT SAUSAGE AND BLACK BEAN CHILI

SERVES 6 TO 8 | PREP TIME: 15 MINUTES | COOK TIME: 9 HOURS

A crockpot soup is a wonderful thing to come home to. Your house will smell delightful when you step in the door and dinner will be ready. Sausages cook well in the slow cooker, but they must be browned first or they may release too much fat into the recipe. This hearty chili uses black beans and lots of vegetables for a delicious meal. It's great served with heated corn tortillas or cornbread hot from the oven.

1 pound Beef Chili Con Carne Sausage (page 53)

2 onions, chopped

6 garlic cloves, minced

2 jalapeño peppers, minced

2 chipotle chile peppers in adobo sauce, minced

1 teaspoon dried oregano

2 (15-ounce) cans black beans, rinsed and drained

1 tablespoon chili powder

5 cups beef stock

1 (14-ounce) can diced tomatoes, undrained

1 (16-ounce) bottle tomato salsa

1 teaspoon salt

¼ teaspoon freshly ground black pepper

3 tablespoons cornstarch

½ cup water

1. Heat a large skillet over medium heat. Add the sausages and cook, turning occasionally with tongs, until they are cooked through.

2. Remove the sausages from the skillet and cut into 1-inch pieces.

3. Add the onions and garlic to the drippings in the skillet and cook until crisp-tender, about 4 minutes.

4. Combine the remaining ingredients except for the cornstarch and water in a 6-quart slow cooker.

5. Cover and cook on low for 8 to 9 hours.

6. Just before you're ready to eat, combine the cornstarch and water in a small bowl and mix well.

7. Stir the cornstarch mixture into the chili. Turn the heat to high.

8. Cover and cook the chili for 15 to 20 minutes until thickened, then serve.

COTECHINO AND BEAN SOUP

SERVES 6 | PREP TIME: 15 MINUTES | COOK TIME: 35 MINUTES

Cotechino is an Italian pork sausage that is very similar to salami. It's delicious in a hearty bean soup, rich with lots of herbs and vegetables. For extra interest and texture, you might want to add orzo pasta to this recipe. You can also serve the soup sprinkled with some freshly grated Parmesan or Romano cheese.

2 tablespoons olive oil

1 pound Cotechino (page 79)

1 leek, chopped

3 garlic cloves, minced

2 sweet potatoes, peeled and cut into chunks

1 (14-ounce) can diced tomatoes, undrained

4 cups chicken stock

2 (15-ounce) cans cannellini beans, drained and rinsed

2 small red chile peppers, diced

1 teaspoon salt

⅛ teaspoon freshly ground black pepper

⅛ teaspoon freshly ground white pepper

1 teaspoon dried basil

1 stalk fresh rosemary, cut into 2-inch pieces

1 bay leaf

1. In a large soup pot or Dutch oven, heat the olive oil over medium heat.

2. Add the sausages and cook, turning occasionally with tongs, until they are cooked through and browned.

3. Remove the sausages and place on paper towels to drain. Cut into 1-inch pieces and set aside (optional).

4. Add the leek and garlic to the drippings in the pot and cook over medium heat, stirring often, until they are crisp-tender, about 4 minutes.

5. Add the remaining ingredients, including the sausages, to the pot.

6. Bring the soup to a boil, then reduce the heat to low and simmer for 20 to 25 minutes, or until the vegetables are tender.

7. Remove and discard the rosemary stems and bay leaf before serving.

Bratwurst, page 59

LENTIL AND BRATWURST SOUP

SERVES 6 | PREP TIME: 15 MINUTES | COOK TIME: 1 HOUR 10 MINUTES

Lentils are dried legumes, but they cook quickly. They have a wonderful soft texture that pairs beautifully with spicy bratwurst. This soup uses green lentils, but you can use brown lentils if you'd like. Before you use them, sort through them to remove any small sticks or stones, then rinse. This soup is great served with breadsticks and beer.

1 pound green lentils

2 tablespoons olive oil

1 pound Bratwurst (page 59)

2 onions, chopped

3 garlic cloves, minced

1 (8-ounce) package cremini mushrooms, sliced

4 large carrots, peeled and sliced

3 tablespoons tomato paste

6 cups chicken stock

1 teaspoon salt

⅛ teaspoon freshly ground black pepper

1 teaspoon dried thyme

1. Sort the lentils and rinse, then drain and set aside.

2. In a large Dutch oven or soup pot, heat the olive oil over medium heat.

3. Add the sausage and cook, turning occasionally with tongs, until cooked through.

4. Remove the sausages and place on paper towels to drain. Cut into 1-inch pieces.

5. Add the onions and garlic to the drippings in the pot. Cook, stirring frequently, until tender, about 6 minutes.

6. Add the mushrooms and carrots to the pot and cook, stirring occasionally, for another 4 minutes.

7. Add the remaining ingredients, including the lentils and reserved sausages, and bring to a simmer over medium heat.

8. Reduce the heat to low and simmer, uncovered, for 50 to 60 minutes, or until the lentils and vegetables are tender.

9. Stir the soup again and serve.

BOCKWURST AND CAULIFLOWER CHOWDER

SERVES 6 | PREP TIME: 15 MINUTES | COOK TIME: 40 MINUTES

Bockwurst is a mild German sausage that pairs well with mild vegetables such as cauliflower. Because the sausage is tender, we will cook it first and then stir it in at the end of the recipe. The sausage drippings add lots of flavor to this recipe. This chowder is rich and thick, making it perfect for a cold fall or winter evening. If you'd like, you can partially purée some of the vegetables in this soup for a creamier texture.

2 tablespoons butter (¼ stick)

1 pound Bockwurst (page 58)

2 onions, chopped

4 garlic cloves, minced

3 large carrots, peeled and sliced

5 tablespoons flour

1 teaspoon salt

1 teaspoon dried marjoram

⅛ teaspoon freshly ground white pepper

6 cups chicken stock

1 large head cauliflower

1 cup light cream

1½ cups shredded Swiss or Havarti cheese

1. Melt the butter in a large soup pot or Dutch oven over medium heat.

2. Add the Bockwurst to the pot and cook, turning occasionally with tongs, until the sausages are cooked through.

3. Remove the sausages from the pot and place them on paper towels to drain. Cut into 1-inch pieces and set aside.

4. Add the onions, garlic, and carrots to the drippings in the pot and cook over medium heat for 5 minutes, until the vegetables are crisp-tender.

5. Add the flour, salt, marjoram, and pepper to the pot and cook, stirring frequently, for 3 to 4 minutes to cook the flour.

6. Add the chicken stock to the pot and bring to a simmer.

7. While the pot simmers, remove the leaves from the cauliflower, remove the core, and roughly chop the florets.

8. Add the cauliflower to the soup.

9. Bring to a simmer again, reduce the heat, and simmer for 15 to 20 minutes, or until the cauliflower is tender.

10. Add the cream, cheese, and cooked sausage to the soup.

11. Heat over medium heat until the soup is steaming and the cheese melts, but don't let it simmer.

12. Serve immediately.

PESTO SAUSAGE VEGETABLE STEW

SERVES 4 | PREP TIME: 15 MINUTES | COOK TIME: 1 HOUR 10 MINUTES

A stew is thicker than soup but doesn't contain dairy or cheese like a chowder. This recipe has lots of different vegetables that are cut into fairly large pieces. The root vegetables release their starch into the chicken stock as they cook, which helps thicken the stew. Pesto, made with basil, garlic, and Parmesan cheese, is the perfect finishing touch to this recipe. It's stirred into the soup just before serving, and offered as a garnish.

3 tablespoons olive oil

1 pound Luganega (page 80)

2 onions, chopped

4 garlic cloves, minced

3 large carrots, peeled and sliced

2 large tomatoes, chopped

2 large parsnips, peeled and chopped

3 large russet potatoes, peeled and chopped

5 cups chicken stock

1 teaspoon salt

1 teaspoon dried basil

⅛ teaspoon freshly ground black pepper

1 (9-ounce) container basil pesto

¼ cup grated Parmesan cheese (optional)

1. In a large soup pot or Dutch oven, heat the olive oil over medium heat.

2. Add the sausages to the pan and cook, turning occasionally with tongs, until they are cooked through.

3. Remove the sausages to paper towels to drain, then cut into 2-inch pieces. Set aside.

4. Add the onions, garlic, and carrots to the drippings in the pot and cook, stirring, until the vegetables are crisp-tender, about 5 minutes.

5. Add the tomatoes, parsnips, potatoes, chicken stock, salt, basil, and pepper and bring to a simmer.

6. Return the sausages to the soup and simmer, uncovered, for 50 to 60 minutes, or until the vegetables are tender.

7. Stir half the pesto into the soup. Offer the remaining pesto as a garnish, along with the Parmesan cheese (if using).

SHRIMP AND FILIPINO SAUSAGE CHOWDER

SERVES 6 | PREP TIME: 15 MINUTES | COOK TIME: 1 HOUR

Longanisa is a sausage that adds a lot of wonderful flavor to this chowder. It's delicious paired with shrimp, an ingredient that is always good with flavorful and slightly salty meats. This chowder would be perfect served with a kale salad dressed with an Italian vinaigrette and tossed with fresh mushrooms. Add hot cornbread or breadsticks on the side for a wonderful dinner.

2 tablespoons butter (¼ stick)

1 pound Filipino Longanisa (page 88)

½ cup water

1 onion, chopped

3 garlic cloves, minced

4 celery stalks, sliced

3 large carrots, peeled and chopped

3 tablespoons flour

1 teaspoon salt

⅛ teaspoon freshly ground black pepper

2 russet potatoes, peeled and chopped

2 cups frozen corn

5 cups chicken stock

1 pound medium raw shrimp, peeled and deveined

1 cup heavy cream

1½ cups shredded Gouda cheese

1. In a large soup pot or Dutch oven, melt the butter over medium heat.

2. Prick the sausages with a fork and add to the pot. Add the water.

3. Bring to a simmer until the water evaporates, then continue cooking, turning occasionally with tongs, until the sausages are browned.

4. Remove the sausages from the pot and place on paper towels to drain. Cut into 1-inch pieces and set aside.

5. Add the onion, garlic, celery, and carrots to the drippings in the pot. Cook, stirring occasionally, over medium heat until the vegetables are crisp-tender, about 4 minutes.

6. Add the flour, salt, and pepper to the vegetables and cook, stirring, for 3 minutes.

continued

SHRIMP AND FILIPINO SAUSAGE CHOWDER *continued*

7. Add the potatoes, corn, and chicken stock and bring to a simmer.

8. Reduce the heat to low and simmer for 30 to 40 minutes, or until the vegetables are tender.

9. Add the shrimp and sausages to the soup. Simmer for 4 to 7 minutes, or until the shrimp curl and turn pink.

10. Add the cream and Gouda cheese. Heat over medium heat until the chowder is steaming and thickened, but do not let it boil. Serve immediately.

FRENCH ONION-SAUSAGE SOUP

SERVES 4 | PREP TIME: 20 MINUTES | COOK TIME: 1 HOUR 10 MINUTES

French onion soup is a classic recipe made from caramelized onions, beef stock, toasted French bread, and lots of cheese. Why not pep up this recipe with some sausages? This soup really is a meal in itself; don't serve it as a first course unless you are serving it in tiny bowls. It's hearty, filling, and absolutely delicious. It should be served with a plain green salad tossed with a vinaigrette dressing, alongside red wine.

3 tablespoons butter

1 pound Lorne (page 68)

4 onions, thinly sliced

5 garlic cloves, minced

5 cups beef stock

½ teaspoon salt

⅛ teaspoon freshly ground black pepper

1 fresh thyme sprig

1 bay leaf

4 thick slices French bread

2 cups shredded Gruyère or Swiss cheese

1. Melt the butter in a soup pot over medium heat.

2. Add the sausages to the pot and cook, until browned and cooked through, about 7 to 9 minutes.

3. Remove the sausages from the pot and set aside.

4. Add the onions to the pot and cook over medium-low heat, stirring often, until the onions are light golden brown and caramelized. This should take about 30 to 40 minutes.

5. Add the garlic to the pot and cook, stirring frequently, until fragrant.

6. Add the beef stock, salt, pepper, thyme, and bay leaf to the pot and stir.

7. Bring to a simmer, then reduce the heat to low and simmer for 20 minutes.

continued ➡

8. Remove the thyme stem and bay leaf from the soup and discard. Add the sausage. Bring to a simmer again.

9. Prepare 4 ovenproof soup bowls and set the oven to broil.

10. Toast the bread slices until golden.

11. Spoon the soup into the bowls and top with the bread and the cheese.

12. Carefully put the bowls onto a heavy baking sheet and broil about 5 inches from the heat, until the cheese melts and is golden brown.

13. Let the bowls stand for 10 to 15 minutes to cool a bit, then serve.

BUFFALO SAUSAGE CHOWDER

SERVES 6 | PREP TIME: 20 MINUTES | COOK TIME: 35 MINUTES

In this recipe, "buffalo" refers to the flavors of buffalo chicken wings. That means spicy. Buffalo wings sauce is made with hot sauce, butter, Worcestershire sauce, and cayenne pepper, and it's just fabulous. It's used in this rich and thick soup along with veggies and, of course, a flavorful sausage. This soup is wonderful served with homemade scones or cornbread, and iced tea or beer.

2 tablespoons butter (¼ stick)

1 tablespoon olive oil

1 pound Garlic Sausage (page 57)

1 large onion, chopped

4 garlic cloves, minced

2 carrots, peeled and sliced

1 cup chopped celery

¼ cup flour

1 teaspoon salt

⅛ teaspoon freshly ground black pepper

1 teaspoon smoked paprika

6 cups chicken stock

1 cup heavy cream

½ cup buffalo wings sauce

½ teaspoon hot sauce

½ cup grated Parmesan cheese, for garnish

1 cup sour cream, for garnish

¼ cup chopped chives, for garnish

1. In a large soup pot or Dutch oven, melt the butter and olive oil over medium heat.

2. Add the sausages and cook, turning occasionally with tongs, until they are cooked through and browned.

3. Remove the sausages from the pot and place on paper towels to drain. Cut the sausages into 1-inch pieces and set aside.

4. Add the onion and garlic to the pot and sauté for 4 minutes, stirring frequently.

5. Add the carrots and celery to the pot and sauté for another 2 minutes.

6. Sprinkle the flour, salt, pepper, and paprika into the pot. Cook over medium heat, stirring often, for 3 minutes.

7. Add the chicken stock and bring to a simmer. Partially cover the pot and simmer for 20 minutes, or until the vegetables are tender.

continued →

BUFFALO SAUSAGE CHOWDER *continued*

8. Return the sausages to the pot and add the cream, buffalo wings sauce, and hot sauce.

9. Stir and heat until the mixture simmers, but do not boil.

10. Serve garnished with the cheese, sour cream, and chives.

CREOLE SOUP

SERVES 6 | PREP TIME: 15 MINUTES | COOK TIME: 45 MINUTES

Chaurice is a spicy pork sausage used in Creole cooking. This type of cooking started in Louisiana and is a combination of several cuisines, combining French, Spanish, Italian, and Haitian flavors and ingredients. The Creole people descended from settlers in the French part of Louisiana. The cuisine is very flavorful—and this soup is no different.

2 tablespoons olive oil

1 pound Chaurice (page 50)

1 onion, chopped

1 leek, chopped

2 celery stalks, sliced

4 garlic cloves, minced

2 (14-ounce) cans diced tomatoes, undrained

6 cups chicken stock

2 teaspoons smoked paprika

1 teaspoon salt

½ teaspoon dried oregano

¼ teaspoon cayenne pepper

1 bay leaf

½ pound medium raw shrimp, peeled and deveined

1. In a large soup pot or Dutch oven, heat the olive oil over medium heat.

2. Add the sausages to the pan and cook, turning occasionally with tongs, until they are cooked through and browned.

3. Remove the sausages and place on paper towels to drain. Cut into 1-inch pieces and set aside.

4. Add the onion, leek, celery, and garlic to the drippings in the pot and cook over medium heat, stirring frequently, until the vegetables are crisp-tender, about 5 minutes.

5. Add the tomatoes, chicken stock, paprika, salt, oregano, cayenne, and bay leaf to the soup.

6. Bring to a simmer, reduce the heat to low, and simmer for 20 minutes.

7. Remove the bay leaf and discard.

8. Add the shrimp and sausage to the soup and simmer over medium heat for 4 to 7 minutes, or until the shrimp curl and turn pink. Serve immediately.

CLAM AND CHORIZO STEW

SERVES 6 | PREP TIME: 15 MINUTES | COOK TIME: 45 MINUTES

Chorizo has a natural affinity with seafood. Clams are inherently sweet and buttery, and are a perfect complement to the sausage and the rest of the ingredients in this hearty stew. Fresh chorizo comes from Mexico, while Spanish chorizo is often dried and cured. You can use either type in this recipe. If you use Mexican chorizo, remove it from its casings to cook; the Spanish chorizo is sliced before cooking.

2 tablespoons olive oil

1 pound chorizo, either Spanish (page 74) or Mexican (page 84)

2 onions, chopped

3 garlic cloves, minced

2 chipotle chile peppers in adobo sauce, minced

½ cup dry white wine

1 (14-ounce) can diced tomatoes, undrained

5 cups chicken or seafood stock

1 bay leaf

1 teaspoon salt

⅛ teaspoon freshly ground black pepper

3 slices cracked-wheat bread, cubed

3 pounds littleneck clams, scrubbed

1. Heat the olive oil in a large soup pot or Dutch oven over medium heat.

2. If you're using the Mexican chorizo, remove it from the casings. Add the sausage to the pot and cook until browned, stirring often, about 6 to 9 minutes. If you're using the Spanish chorizo, slice it and cook until it is crisp around the edges, stirring often, about 5 to 7 minutes.

3. Remove the sausage from the skillet and place it on paper towels to drain.

4. Add the onions, garlic, and chiles in adobo sauce to the skillet, and cook over medium heat until tender, about 4 to 5 minutes.

5. Add the wine. Cook, stirring frequently, until it has almost evaporated.

6. Add the tomatoes, chicken stock, bay leaf, salt, and pepper and bring to a simmer. Simmer the soup for 20 minutes over medium-low heat.

7. Add the bread and sausage to the soup and simmer for another 10 minutes, or until the bread has thickened the soup.

8. Add the clams to the soup and cover. Cook for 2 to 4 minutes, shaking the pot occasionally, until the clams open.

9. Remove and discard the bay leaf and any clams that do not open. Serve immediately.

ENTRÉES

CH. 11

In this chapter, you'll find some truly imaginative recipes for weeknight favorites that highlight the versatility of sausage. Salads, stir-fries, pizzas, pastas, and more all get the star treatment. Indulge in a kicked-up version of the Windy City claim to fame, Deep-Dish Sausage Pizza, featuring Hot Italian Sausage (page 78). Wash it down with a crisp pilsner. Equally good with a fresh cold one are the Bacon Cheeseburger Sausage Sliders, which are incredibly easy to make. Or try the Hot German Potato Salad, inspired by Wurstsalat, a classic German dish.

SAUSAGE RISOTTO

SERVES 4 | PREP TIME: 15 MINUTES | COOK TIME: 25 MINUTES

Risotto, a classic Italian dish, is made with short-grain rice that releases starch as it cooks, making the finished product creamy and rich. Adding sausage to this recipe makes it heartier and more like a meal. You can use any sausage in this recipe; pick one you think blends well with cheese, mushrooms, and rice. Serve alongside some white wine and a fruit salad.

2 tablespoons olive oil

1 pound Ćevapi (page 85)

1 onion, chopped

4 garlic cloves, minced

1 (8-ounce) package cremini
    mushrooms, sliced

6 cups chicken stock

2 cups short-grain Arborio rice

⅓ cup dry white wine

1 teaspoon dried marjoram

1 teaspoon salt

⅛ teaspoon freshly ground black pepper

2 cups chopped kale

⅔ cup grated Parmesan cheese

2 tablespoons butter (¼ stick)

1. Heat the olive oil in a large skillet over medium heat.

2. Remove the sausages from the casings and crumble into the skillet. Cook over medium heat, stirring frequently, until the sausage is browned.

3. When the sausage is cooked, remove from the skillet with a slotted spoon and set aside.

4. Add the onion, garlic, and mushrooms to the skillet and sauté until tender, about 4 to 5 minutes.

5. Meanwhile, pour the chicken stock into a medium saucepan and place over low heat.

6. Add the rice to the skillet and stir for 2 minutes, until the rice is coated with the oil and drippings.

7. Add the wine, marjoram, salt, and pepper to the skillet. Cook and stir until the rice absorbs the wine.

8. Add the warm chicken stock to the rice mixture about ½ cup at a time, stirring frequently. Continue adding stock until the rice absorbs it and becomes al dente. The mixture will become creamy as the rice cooks.

9. When the rice is tender, add the kale, Parmesan cheese, cooked sausage, and butter and stir gently. Cover the skillet and remove from the heat.

10. Let stand for 5 minutes, then stir the risotto again and serve.

SHRIMP AND CHAO TOM STIR-FRY

SERVES 4 | PREP TIME: 15 MINUTES | COOK TIME: 20 MINUTES

This elegant stir-fry uses two kinds of shrimp: whole shrimp and shrimp sausage. Fresh herbs add a punch of flavor. Mint and basil may seem like an unusual combination, but this pairing is often used in Vietnamese cooking. When you stir-fry make sure you have all of the ingredients ready before you start cooking. Serve this recipe over hot jasmine rice with a cold beer on the side.

2 tablespoons peanut oil

1 pound Vietnamese Shrimp Sausage (page 87)

1 bunch green onions, sliced

2 garlic cloves, minced

1 stalk lemongrass, bent

½ pound fresh green beans, cut into 1-inch pieces

1 cup chicken or seafood stock

1 tablespoon fish sauce

1 tablespoon cornstarch

1 pound fresh medium raw shrimp, peeled and deveined

1 tablespoon freshly squeezed lime juice

1 tablespoon chopped fresh basil

1 tablespoon chopped fresh mint

⅛ teaspoon cayenne pepper

1. In a wok or large skillet, heat the peanut oil over medium heat. Add the sausages and cook until firm, turning occasionally with tongs, about 5 to 8 minutes.

2. Remove the sausages from the wok and cut into 1½-inch pieces, and set aside.

3. Add the green onions, garlic, and lemongrass to the wok. Stir-fry over medium heat until fragrant, about 3 minutes.

4. Add the green beans to the wok and stir-fry for 4 minutes more. Remove and discard the lemongrass.

5. Combine the chicken stock, fish sauce, and cornstarch in a small bowl and mix well.

6. Add the stock mixture to the wok along with the sausages. Bring to a simmer.

7. Add the shrimp and stir-fry until they curl and turn pink.

8. Add the lime juice, basil, mint, and cayenne to the wok and stir-fry for 1 to 2 minutes more, then serve immediately.

LINCOLNSHIRE SAUSAGE SPINACH PIE

SERVES 4 | PREP TIME: 20 MINUTES | COOK TIME: 1 HOUR 15 MINUTES

This two-crust pie is a real showstopper. The filling is made from three kinds of cheese, plus eggs, cooked onion, mushrooms, garlic, and spinach, and it has bits of sausage nestled throughout. It's a great recipe for entertaining, and perfect for a cool fall night. Let the pie stand for 10 minutes before slicing so the filling firms up a bit and you can cut perfect slices. Serve with a fruit salad and white wine.

2 tablespoons butter (¼ stick)

1 pound Lincolnshire Sausage (page 66)

1 onion, chopped

3 garlic cloves, minced

1 (8-ounce) package cremini mushrooms, sliced

½ pound fresh spinach, rinsed and dried

1 (8-ounce) package cream cheese, softened

5 eggs

2 cups shredded mozzarella cheese

1 cup shredded Gruyère cheese

1 cup shredded Monterey Jack cheese

2 pie crust dough rounds

1 tablespoon milk

1. Preheat the oven to 375°F.

2. In a large skillet, melt the butter over medium heat.

3. Add the sausages to the skillet and cook, turning occasionally with tongs, until cooked through and browned, about 8 minutes.

4. Remove the sausages from the skillet and place on paper towels to drain. Cut into 1-inch pieces and set aside.

5. Add the onion, garlic, and mushrooms to the skillet. Cook, while stirring, until the mushrooms give up their liquid and the liquid evaporates.

6. Add the spinach to the skillet and cook until wilted, about 4 minutes.

7. In a large bowl, beat the cream cheese until fluffy. Add the eggs, one at a time, beating after each addition, until smooth.

continued →

8. Stir in all of the cheeses.

9. Then stir in the sausage pieces and the vegetables.

10. Line a 9-inch pie plate with one of the pie crusts. Spoon the filling into the crust.

11. Top with the remaining pie crust. Seal and crimp the edges. Cut some slits in the top crust to let the steam escape.

12. Brush the top crust with milk.

13. Bake the pie for 50 to 60 minutes, or until the top crust is golden brown.

14. Let the pie stand for 10 minutes before slicing to serve.

HOT GERMAN POTATO SALAD

SERVES 4 | PREP TIME: 10 MINUTES | COOK TIME: 35 MINUTES

Hot German Potato Salad is completely different from cold potato salad. Here, savory sausage and tender potatoes are enveloped in a warm sweet-and-sour sauce. I like serving this with a green salad tossed with ranch salad dressing and toasted garlic bread. Beer or wine would be great accompaniments as well.

6 large russet potatoes

3 tablespoons butter

1 pound Weisswurst (page 60)

1 onion, chopped

4 garlic cloves, minced

2 tablespoons flour

1 tablespoon cornstarch

½ cup apple cider vinegar

3 tablespoons freshly squeezed lemon juice

1 cup chicken stock

¼ cup sugar

¼ cup honey

2 tablespoons Dijon mustard

⅓ cup sour cream

1. Bring a large pot of water to a boil. Cook the potatoes until tender, about 10 to 15 minutes. Drain and set aside.

2. In the same large pot, melt the butter over medium heat.

3. Add the sausages to the pot and cook, turning occasionally with tongs, until they are cooked through and browned. Remove the sausages from the pot and place on paper towels to drain. Cut into 2-inch pieces and set aside.

4. Add the onion and garlic to the drippings in the pot. Cook, stirring frequently, for 5 to 6 minutes, or until tender.

5. Add the flour and cornstarch to the pot and cook, while stirring, until bubbly, about 2 minutes.

6. Add the apple cider vinegar, lemon juice, chicken stock, sugar, and honey to the pot and bring to a simmer.

7. Add the potatoes and sausages to the pot and simmer for 5 minutes more.

8. Stir in the mustard and sour cream and heat until steaming. Serve immediately.

DEEP-DISH SAUSAGE PIZZA

SERVES 6 | PREP TIME: 30 MINUTES, PLUS 1 HOUR TO LET RISE | COOK TIME: 1 HOUR

There's nothing like a homemade pizza to put any takeout or frozen pizza to shame. Homemade yeast dough is more flavorful and tender than any other type, and with your own homemade sausage, this is a feast. Deep-dish pizza is just pizza with more filling. The pizza is usually made in a 10-inch springform pan or an ovenproof skillet. This pizza is meant to be eaten with a fork and knife. Pair it with a fruit salad for a great meal.

1½ cups all-purpose flour

½ cup whole-wheat flour

1 (¼-ounce) package dry yeast

1 teaspoon sugar

½ teaspoon salt

¼ cup olive oil

½ cup warm water

1 pound Hot Italian Sausage (page 78)

1 onion, chopped

4 garlic cloves, minced

1 red bell pepper, chopped

4 Roma tomatoes, chopped

1 (6-ounce) can tomato paste

⅓ cup water

1 teaspoon dried Italian seasoning

½ teaspoon dried basil

2 cups shredded mozzarella cheese

1 cup shredded Monterey Jack cheese

2 tablespoons grated Parmesan cheese

1. In a medium bowl, combine the all-purpose flour, whole-wheat flour, yeast, sugar, and salt.

2. Add the olive oil and warm water and stir to make a dough.

3. Knead the dough on a floured surface for 5 minutes. Put the dough in a greased bowl, slide the dough over to one side, and turn it upside down to make sure that the top is also greased. Cover with a towel and let stand for 1 hour until it doubles in size.

4. While the dough rises, remove the sausages from their casings.

5. Brown the sausage in a large skillet over medium heat, stirring occasionally, until it's almost cooked.

6. Add the onion and garlic to the pan and cook, stirring frequently, for 5 minutes more, or until the sausage is browned and the vegetables are tender.

7. Drain it if there is a lot of fat in the pan.

8. Add the bell pepper, tomatoes, tomato paste, water, Italian seasoning, and basil. Bring to a simmer.

9. Simmer for 10 minutes.

10. To assemble the pizza, first preheat the oven to 425°F.

11. Punch down the dough and roll it out on a floured surface to a 12-inch circle.

12. Put the dough in a greased 10-inch springform pan or oven-proof skillet, letting the dough reach 1 inch up the sides of the pan for a crust.

13. Sprinkle the bottom of the dough with ⅔ cup of the mozzarella cheese. Spread the meat sauce on top of the cheese. Sprinkle with the remaining mozzarella cheese, Monterey Jack cheese, and Parmesan cheese.

14. Bake the pizza for 30 to 40 minutes, or until the crust is deep golden brown and the cheese is melted and browned in spots.

15. Loosen the edges of the pan and remove the pan sides. Slice into wedges to serve.

SALMON AND SPANISH CHORIZO BAKE

SERVES 4 | PREP TIME: 10 MINUTES | COOK TIME: 18 MINUTES

This flavorful and elegant dinner is a one-pan meal. As a result, the sausage flavors the fish and all of the vegetables. You can make this recipe with any type of fish you like. Because most fish cooks quicker than salmon (which takes about 10 minutes per inch of thickness), just adjust the cooking time accordingly. Serve with a mixed greens salad tossed with avocado and mushrooms.

1 pound Spanish Chorizo (page 74)

1 red onion, sliced

1 (8-ounce) package button mushrooms, sliced

1 pound asparagus

4 (6-ounce) salmon fillets

2 tablespoons olive oil

1 teaspoon salt

⅛ teaspoon freshly ground black pepper

1. Preheat the oven to 425°F.

2. Prick the sausages with a fork.

3. Arrange the sausages, onion, mushrooms, asparagus, and salmon on a heavy 15-by-10-inch pan.

4. Drizzle with the olive oil and sprinkle with the salt and pepper.

5. Roast for 13 to 18 minutes, or until the salmon is cooked through and the vegetables are crisp-tender. Serve immediately.

BÁNH MÌ AND SHRIMP WITH BROWN BUTTER RICE

SERVES 6 | PREP TIME: 20 MINUTES | COOK TIME: 50 MINUTES

Bánh mì is a Vietnamese sandwich made with pickled vegetables and a spicy mayonnaise. It usually includes roast pork and pâté. But by using our Vietnamese Chicken Sausage, we can make a simpler version. You get all of the flavors of the classic bánh mì sandwich without the work. In this recipe, shrimp and veggies are stir-fried with the sausage, then the whole thing is served over rice mixed with brown butter.

1 cup jasmine or basmati rice

3 cups chicken stock, divided

3 tablespoons butter

2 tablespoons peanut or safflower oil

1 pound Vietnamese Chicken
 Sausage (page 89)

2 shallots, minced

2 garlic cloves, minced

1 tablespoon grated fresh ginger

1 cup shredded carrots

1 cup shredded cucumber

¼ cup shredded daikon radish

1 pound medium raw shrimp, peeled
 and deveined

2 tablespoons soy sauce

2 tablespoons freshly squeezed lime juice

2 tablespoons cornstarch

1 teaspoon toasted sesame oil

¼ cup chopped fresh cilantro

1. In a medium saucepan, combine the rice and 2 cups of chicken stock and bring to a boil.

2. Reduce the heat to low, cover, and simmer for 15 to 20 minutes, or until the rice is tender and has absorbed the liquid.

3. Meanwhile, brown the butter in a small saucepan over medium-low heat, about 10 to 15 minutes. Watch the butter carefully so it doesn't burn. When the butter turns golden brown, remove from the heat.

4. When the rice is tender, stir in the browned butter and set aside. Keep warm.

5. In a wok or large skillet, heat the peanut oil over medium heat.

6. Add the sausages to the skillet and cook until they are cooked through and browned, about 8 to 10 minutes.

continued →

7. Remove the sausages and cut into 1-inch pieces.

8. Add the shallots, garlic, ginger, and carrots to the oil remaining in the wok. Stir-fry for 4 to 5 minutes until crisp-tender.

9. Add the cucumber and radish to the wok and stir-fry for another 2 to 3 minutes.

10. Add the shrimp to the wok and stir-fry just until the shrimp curl and turn pink, another 2 to 3 minutes. Add the sausages to the wok.

11. In a small bowl, mix the soy sauce, lime juice, cornstarch, and the remaining 1 cup of chicken stock, and add the mixture to the wok. Stir-fry until thickened.

12. Add the sesame oil and fresh cilantro and toss. Serve immediately over the rice.

ITALIAN WEDDING CASSEROLE

SERVES 8 | PREP TIME: 15 MINUTES | COOK TIME: 50 MINUTES

Italian wedding soup is a classic recipe from that country, and it has nothing to do with weddings. The name refers to the combination of meat and greens in the recipe. This recipe turns the soup into a casserole and adds a little bit of spice. Many recipes for the traditional soup use chicken meatballs, so chicken sausage is a natural substitute. Serve this with a mixed greens salad tossed with Italian dressing.

Nonstick cooking spray

1 (16-ounce) package bow tie pasta

2 tablespoons olive oil

1 pound White Chili Chicken Sausage (page 52)

1 onion, chopped

3 garlic cloves, minced

3 tablespoons flour

1 teaspoon dried Italian seasoning

1 teaspoon salt

⅛ teaspoon freshly ground white pepper

1 cup chicken stock

1½ cups whole milk

1 cup grated provolone cheese

½ cup grated Parmesan cheese

1 (10-ounce) bag baby spinach

1 (16-ounce) package frozen baby peas

¼ cup grated Romano cheese

1. Preheat the oven to 350°F. Spray a 9-by-13-inch glass baking dish with nonstick cooking spray and set aside.

2. Bring a large pot of salted water to a boil.

3. Cook the pasta according to package directions until al dente. Drain and set aside.

4. In a large skillet, heat the olive oil over medium heat. Add the sausages and cook, turning occasionally with tongs, until they are cooked through and browned. Remove from the skillet and cut into 1-inch pieces.

5. Add the onion and garlic to the skillet. Cook and stir until tender, about 5 minutes.

6. Add the flour, Italian seasoning, salt, and pepper to the skillet. Cook and stir for 2 minutes.

continued →

7. Add the chicken stock and milk to the skillet. Cook, stirring with a wire whisk, until the sauce is thickened and smooth.

8. Add the provolone and Parmesan cheese to the sauce along with the sausages, spinach, and peas. Cook, stirring occasionally, until the spinach has wilted.

9. Pour the mixture into the prepared baking dish and top with the Romano cheese.

10. Bake for 30 to 40 minutes, or until the casserole is bubbling and lightly browned on top.

THE BEST LASAGNA

SERVES 8 | PREP TIME: 20 MINUTES, PLUS OVERNIGHT TO CHILL | COOK TIME: 1 HOUR 40 MINUTES

Everyone has a favorite lasagna recipe. But this one is something special. It uses two types of sausage and four kinds of cheese for fabulous flavor. The noodles aren't cooked ahead of time in this recipe, so it's easier than most. The lasagna sits in the refrigerator overnight so the noodles soften. It's rich and hearty and perfect for feeding a crowd. Serve it with a green salad tossed with croutons and hot cheesy garlic bread.

1 pound Sweet Italian Sausage (page 77)

½ pound Garlic Sausage (page 57)

2 onions, chopped

1 leek, chopped

3 garlic cloves, minced

½ cup finely grated carrots

2 (14-ounce) cans diced tomatoes, undrained

1 (8-ounce) can tomato sauce

1 (6-ounce) can tomato paste

½ cup beef stock

1 teaspoon dried Italian seasoning

1 teaspoon dried basil

1 teaspoon salt

⅛ teaspoon freshly ground black pepper

1 cup ricotta cheese

1 (8-ounce) package cream cheese, softened

2 eggs

3 cups shredded mozzarella cheese, divided

Nonstick cooking spray

8 uncooked lasagna noodles

½ cup grated Romano cheese

1. Remove the sausages from their casings. Crumble into a large skillet and put the skillet over medium heat.

2. Add the onions, leek, and garlic to the skillet. Cook, stirring frequently to break up the meat, until the sausage is brown and the vegetables are tender, about 10 minutes.

3. Drain the mixture well.

4. Add the carrots, diced tomatoes, tomato sauce, tomato paste, beef stock, Italian seasoning, basil, salt, and pepper and bring to a simmer over medium heat. Reduce the heat to low and simmer for 20 minutes.

5. While the mixture simmers, combine the ricotta cheese and cream cheese in a medium bowl and beat until well combined.

6. Beat the eggs into the cheese mixture until well combined. Stir in 1 cup of mozzarella cheese.

continued ➡

7. Spray a 9-by-13-inch glass baking dish with nonstick cooking spray.

8. Spread 1 cup of the meat sauce into the bottom of the dish. Top with 4 lasagna noodles. Top the noodles with ½ of the cheese mixture, and then ½ of the remaining sauce. Sprinkle with half of the remaining mozzarella cheese.

9. Repeat these layers again, starting with the lasagna noodles and ending with the remaining mozzarella cheese. Sprinkle the top of the lasagna with Romano cheese.

10. Cover the lasagna with aluminum foil and refrigerate overnight.

11. When you're ready to eat, preheat the oven to 350°F.

12. Bake the lasagna, covered, for 30 minutes. Then remove the foil and bake for 30 to 40 minutes longer, or until the lasagna is bubbling, the noodles are tender (use a fork to check), and the cheese starts to brown on top.

13. Let stand for 20 minutes before slicing to serve.

ENCHILADA STUFFED PEPPERS

SERVES 4 | PREP TIME: 20 MINUTES | COOK TIME: 45 MINUTES

Stuffed peppers are another classic Italian recipe, but this version spices things up with some Mexican flavors. Garlic sausage has intense flavor, and it's delicious paired with sweet red, orange, and yellow bell peppers. You could use different types of rice such as basmati, or even wild rice.

4 large bell peppers of different colors

1 pound Garlic Sausage (page 57)

1 onion, chopped

2 garlic cloves, minced

1 (8-ounce) can enchilada sauce

2 teaspoons chili powder

½ teaspoon ground cumin

½ teaspoon salt

⅛ teaspoon cayenne pepper

1½ cups cooked white or brown rice

1 cup shredded pepper Jack cheese

¼ cup grated Parmesan cheese

¼ cup water

1. Preheat the oven to 350°F. Cut the tops off the bell peppers. Remove the membranes from the insides and set the peppers aside.

2. Remove the sausages from the casings.

3. Brown the sausage with the onion and garlic in a large skillet over medium heat, stirring frequently to break up the meat, until the meat is cooked through and browned. Drain the meat.

4. Return the skillet to the heat and add the enchilada sauce, chili powder, cumin, salt, cayenne, and rice and mix well.

5. Stir in the Jack cheese and take the skillet off the heat.

6. Place the bell peppers in a baking dish so they fit together snugly. Fill the peppers with the sausage mixture.

7. Sprinkle with the Parmesan cheese. Pour ¼ cup of water into the pan around the peppers.

8. Bake for 25 to 35 minutes, or until the peppers are tender and the cheese on top has started to brown.

MOROCCAN PIZZA

SERVES 4 | PREP TIME: 30 MINUTES, PLUS 1 HOUR TO LET RISE | COOK TIME: 40 MINUTES

There's nothing like a hot and crisp pizza, rich with spices, meat, and melting gooey cheese, fresh from the oven. Making your own pizza is a fun way to get the whole family involved! You could make the crust ahead of time, then have everyone join in to roll it out and add the toppings. You can use any cooked sausage in this recipe; just make sure to think about the flavors you like best for fun combinations.

1 cup all-purpose flour

½ cup whole-wheat flour

½ cup bread flour

1 (¼-ounce) package instant dry yeast

½ teaspoon salt

¾ cup warm water

3 tablespoons olive oil, divided

1 pound Merguez (page 76)

1 leek, chopped

2 garlic cloves, minced

1 eggplant, thinly sliced

1 (8-ounce) can tomato sauce

2 tablespoons harissa chili paste

½ teaspoon ground cumin

¼ cup black olive slices

1 cup crumbled firm goat cheese

1. In a medium bowl, combine the all-purpose flour, whole-wheat flour, bread flour, yeast, and salt. Mix well.

2. Add the warm water and 2 tablespoons of olive oil. Mix until a dough forms. (You may need to add more flour or water to achieve a firm but workable dough.)

3. Knead the dough on a floured surface for 5 minutes.

4. Put the dough into a greased bowl, slide the dough over to one side and turn it upside down to make sure that the top is also greased. Cover the bowl with a towel and let rise for 1 hour.

5. While the dough rises, heat the remaining 1 tablespoon of olive oil in a large skillet over medium heat.

6. Add the sausages and cook, turning frequently, until they are cooked through.

7. Remove the sausages from the skillet and place on paper towels to drain, then cut into 1-inch slices.

8. Add the leek and garlic to the drippings in the skillet and cook, stirring frequently, until tender.

9. Add the eggplant slices. Cook, turning the slices occasionally, until tender.

10. Put the tomato sauce, chili paste, and cumin in a small bowl and mix together.

11. When you're ready to make the pizza, preheat the oven to 425°F.

12. Punch down the dough and roll it out on a greased pizza pan or large cookie sheet.

13. Spread the tomato sauce on the dough and top with the eggplant-and-vegetable mixture. Top with the sausage pieces and the olive slices. Sprinkle with the goat cheese.

14. Bake the pizza for 18 to 28 minutes, or until the crust is deep golden brown and the toppings are hot. Cut into wedges to serve.

SAUSAGE WITH PENNE

SERVES 4 | PREP TIME: 15 MINUTES | COOK TIME: 40 MINUTES

Sausages and pasta make a wonderful entrée recipe. Beef bangers are tender sausages that work well in an herbed tomato sauce that is served over tender penne pasta. You can use any type of pasta you'd like in this recipe; ziti, gemelli, spaghetti, or linguine would be delicious. Serve with a green salad tossed with mushrooms, and a hearty red wine.

2 tablespoons olive oil

1 pound Beef Bangers (page 65)

1 onion, chopped

6 garlic cloves, minced

2 red bell peppers, chopped

1 (8-ounce) package button
  mushrooms, sliced

1 (26-ounce) jar marinara sauce

⅓ cup dry red wine or beef stock

¼ cup tomato paste

½ teaspoon salt

1 teaspoon dried basil

1 teaspoon dried oregano

⅛ teaspoon freshly ground black pepper

1 (16-ounce) package penne pasta

½ cup grated Parmesan cheese

1. Heat the olive oil in a large skillet over medium heat.

2. Add the sausages to the skillet and cook, turning occasionally with tongs, until cooked through and browned, about 10 minutes.

3. Remove the sausages from the skillet and cut into 1-inch pieces.

4. Add the onion, garlic, bell peppers, and mushrooms to the drippings in the skillet. Cook over medium heat, stirring frequently, until crisp-tender, about 10 minutes.

5. Add the marinara sauce, wine, tomato paste, salt, basil, oregano, and pepper and bring to a simmer. Simmer over low heat for 20 minutes.

6. Bring a large pot of water to a boil. Cook the penne pasta according to package directions until al dente.

7. Drain the pasta, reserving ⅓ cup of the cooking liquid, and add the pasta to the skillet.

8. Toss the pasta with the sauce, adding cooking liquid as needed, until it is coated.

9. Serve immediately topped with the Parmesan cheese.

CHAURICE SAUSAGE CARBONARA

SERVES 4 | PREP TIME: 10 MINUTES | COOK TIME: 20 MINUTES

Carbonara is a classic Italian recipe that combines cooked pasta with bacon, eggs, and cheese. The eggs are beaten with cream and cheese and stirred into the hot cooked pasta, which cooks the eggs and creates a creamy sauce. Substituting sausage for the bacon is a great choice that adds more flavor and makes this dish heartier. You can remove the sausage from the casings or cook it in the casings and slice it for this recipe.

1 (16-ounce) package spaghetti or linguine pasta

2 tablespoons butter

1 pound Chaurice, whole or removed from the casings (page 50)

1 leek, chopped

3 garlic cloves, minced

4 eggs

⅓ cup heavy cream

3 tablespoons white wine

⅔ cup grated Parmesan cheese, divided

1. Bring a large pot of water to a boil.

2. Cook the pasta according to package directions until al dente. Drain, reserving ½ cup of the cooking liquid.

3. While the pasta cooks, melt the butter over medium heat in a large skillet.

4. Add the sausage, either whole or removed from the casings and crumbled into the pan. Cook until the sausage is thoroughly cooked and browned, about 10 minutes.

5. Remove the sausage from the skillet. Either cut the whole sausages into 1-inch pieces or drain the cooked, crumbled sausage on paper towels.

6. Add the leek and garlic to the pan drippings and cook over medium heat until crisp-tender, about 4 minutes.

continued ⟶

7. Beat the eggs, cream, wine, and ⅓ cup of Parmesan cheese in a medium bowl.

8. Take the skillet off the heat. Add the drained pasta to the leek and garlic in the skillet and immediately add the egg mixture and reserved sausage.

9. Toss the mixture with tongs until the pasta is coated, adding reserved cooking liquid as necessary to form a sauce.

10. Serve immediately with the remaining ⅓ cup of Parmesan cheese.

BACON CHEESEBURGER SAUSAGE SLIDERS

SERVES 4 | PREP TIME: 10 MINUTES | COOK TIME: 15 MINUTES

Sliders are little burgers that kids just love. While this simple recipe is one of the easiest in this collection, it has all the flavor of bacon cheeseburgers, wrapped up in sausages! The only thing to worry about is to make sure the sausages are fully cooked before you assemble the little sandwiches. Dinner rolls are the best choice for buns in this recipe.

1 pound Bacon Cheeseburger Sausage (page 49)

7 tablespoons ketchup

7 tablespoons mustard

7 tablespoons pickle relish

7 tablespoons mayonnaise

10 to 12 small dinner rolls, cut in half

10 to 12 slices American or Swiss cheese

1 head of lettuce, outer leaves discarded

2 Roma tomatoes, sliced

1. Prepare and preheat a gas or charcoal grill.

2. Grill the sausages until they are brown and cooked through, until they reach an internal temperature of at least 165°F.

3. Assemble the sliders with your choice of the toppings on the dinner rolls, and serve.

Weisswurst, page 60

GRILLED WEISSWURST SAUSAGE AND FENNEL SALAD

SERVES 4 | PREP TIME: 15 MINUTES | COOK TIME: 20 MINUTES

A warm salad is a wonderful meal in the early fall, or even on a cool summer evening. This one is something special, because it uses your own homemade weisswurst. The grill adds a fabulous smoky flavor to the fennel and the sausage. A simple dressing and some crumbled feta cheese are perfect complements to complete this meal-in-one. Serve with toasted garlic bread and white wine.

1 head romaine lettuce, cut in half
2 fennel bulbs, trimmed and cut into quarters
2 tablespoons olive oil
1 teaspoon salt
⅛ teaspoon freshly ground black pepper
1 pound Weisswurst (page 60)
4 cups baby spinach leaves
½ cup oil and vinegar salad dressing
⅓ cup crumbled feta cheese

1. Prepare and preheat a gas or charcoal grill.

2. Drizzle the lettuce and fennel with the olive oil and sprinkle with the salt and pepper.

3. Grill the lettuce, cut-side down, for 2 to 3 minutes, or until the lettuce starts to brown. Remove to a plate and set aside.

4. Grill the fennel along with the sausages, turning each frequently, until the fennel is tender with nice grill marks and the sausages are cooked through, about 10 to 15 minutes.

5. Use a sharp knife to chop the lettuce. Combine with the spinach in a large serving bowl. When the sausage is cool enough to handle, cut on an angle into 1-inch pieces.

6. Toss the lettuce with the salad dressing and put on plates.

7. Top the greens with some of the fennel, sausages, and feta cheese. Serve immediately.

CUMBERLAND SAUSAGE AND POTATO KEBABS

SERVES 4 | PREP TIME. 15 MINUTES | COOK TIME. 35 MINUTES

Sausages make fabulous kabobs. The flavorful sausages and tender potatoes are grilled until they are hot and smoky along with tasty vegetables. The potatoes and sausages are partially cooked before they are skewered, and are then finished on the grill. Don't partially cook the sausages ahead of time; cook when you are ready to finish grilling so they retain their heat.

1 pound Cumberland Sausage (page 67)

6 medium red potatoes, cut into 2-inch cubes

½ cup water

2 red bell peppers, cut into 2-inch pieces

1 zucchini, cut into 1-inch pieces

3 tablespoons olive oil

2 tablespoons red wine vinegar

2 tablespoons Dijon mustard

1 teaspoon dried marjoram

1 teaspoon salt

⅛ teaspoon freshly ground black pepper

1. Put the sausages in a large skillet and add the water. Simmer over medium heat until the water evaporates, then let the sausages brown until they are just barely firm. Remove from the heat and cut into 2-inch pieces.

2. While the sausages cook, put the potatoes into a large pot of cold water. Bring to a simmer over high heat, then reduce the heat to low and simmer for 12 to 17 minutes, or until the potatoes are almost tender. Drain well.

3. Using 10- to 12-inch metal skewers, thread the sausage pieces, potatoes, bell peppers, and zucchini.

4. In a small bowl, combine the olive oil, red wine vinegar, mustard, marjoram, salt, and pepper and mix well. Brush this over the kabobs.

5. Prepare and preheat a gas or charcoal grill. Grill the kebabs, covered, over medium coals for 10 to 15 minutes or until the sausages are thoroughly cooked and the vegetables are tender.

SAUCES & CONDIMENTS

CH. 12

The true measure of the quality of a sausage is how good it tastes on its own, but the right condiment can really take your experience to the next level. Condiments can either contrast with the salt, fat, and richness of the sausage, cutting through it and priming you for the next bite, or complement it, heightening the intensity of the herbs, spices, and other seasonings in the mix. In this chapter, you'll find condiments to satisfy every palate. You'll learn just how easy it is to make your own Spicy Mustard—which will make you wonder why you ever bothered with store-bought. You will revel in the versatility of the addictive Bang Bang Sauce, and get a chance to exercise your creativity by experimenting with different beer styles in the recipe for Spicy Beer Sauce. If you're planning on throwing a big party, whip up an assortment of sweet, savory, zesty, and spicy condiments to let everyone mix and match—a guaranteed conversation starter.

SPICY MUSTARD

MAKES 1 CUP | PREP TIME: 15 MINUTES | STANDING TIME: 3 TO 4 DAYS

Good with Bockwurst, page 58, Bacon Cheeseburger Sausage, page 49, Garlic Sausage, page 57, and Fresh Kielbasa, page 56

If you've never made homemade mustard, you'll be surprised at how easy it is. Your own mustard will taste better than anything you can buy in a store. And you can make it as mild or as spicy as you'd like. The mustard should rest for a few days before you use it so the flavors blend and mellow a bit. It tastes great when spread on sausage sandwiches, or combined with sour cream as an appetizer dip.

¾ cup apple cider vinegar

⅓ cup yellow mustard seeds

⅓ cup brown mustard seeds

1 teaspoon ground mustard

1 teaspoon honey

1 teaspoon salt

⅛ teaspoon cayenne pepper

¼ teaspoon turmeric

1 tablespoon water

1. Combine the vinegar and both mustard seeds in a bowl.

2. Cover and let the mixture stand at room temperature for 8 hours.

3. Put the mustard-seed mixture into a blender and add the ground mustard, honey, salt, cayenne, turmeric, and water.

4. Blend the mixture until it is smooth.

5. Pour the mustard into a jar with a tight lid. Seal, and let stand in the refrigerator for 3 to 4 days, stirring every day. This will help mellow the mustard.

6. When the mustard tastes the way you like it, you can use it. Store tightly covered in the refrigerator.

BANG BANG SAUCE

MAKES 1 CUP | PREP TIME: 5 MINUTES | STANDING TIME: 1 HOUR

Good with Classic Pub Bangers, page 64, Garlic Sausage, page 57, Bratwurst, page 59, and Hot Italian Sausage, page 78

Bang Bang Sauce is a mayonnaise-based recipe typically served as a sauce with shrimp and pasta. But it's also a delicious condiment for many different sausages. This sauce is sweet and hot, with quite a kick from adobo sauce and chipotle chiles. Grill a variety of sausages, then serve them with this sauce for a great appetizer, or you can make a meal out of it if you grill some veggies, too.

¾ cup mayonnaise

3 tablespoons Thai sweet chili sauce

2 chipotle chile peppers in adobo
    sauce, minced

2 tablespoons adobo sauce

1 garlic clove, finely minced

2 tablespoons honey

1 teaspoon freshly squeezed lime juice

1. Combine all of the ingredients in a small bowl and mix well.

2. Cover the bowl and refrigerate for 1 hour to blend the flavors.

3. Store in the refrigerator, tightly covered, for up to 6 days.

HONEY MUSTARD

MAKES 1 CUP | PREP TIME: 10 MINUTES

Good with Rosemary-Lamb Sausage, page 46, Bockwurst, page 58,
Lincolnshire Sausage, page 66, Cumberland Sausage, page 67,
and Beef Bangers, page 65

Honey mustard became popular about 30 years ago, and it remains a favorite condiment to use with grilled or broiled sausages. The combination of sweet honey with sharp and tangy mustard really brings out the flavor of the sausages. You can use your favorite mustard in this recipe—perhaps your own homemade Spicy Mustard (page 166)—and it will be delicious. Keep it in the refrigerator, tightly covered, for up to 1 month.

½ cup mustard

⅓ cup honey

1 tablespoon mayonnaise or sour cream

1 tablespoon freshly squeezed lemon juice

1. Combine all of the ingredients in a small bowl and blend well with a wire whisk.

2. Store, covered, in the refrigerator for up to 1 month.

JALAPEÑO MUSTARD SAUCE

MAKES 1 CUP | PREP TIME: 10 MINUTES

*Good with White Chili Chicken Sausage, page 52, Garlic Sausage, page 57,
Chaurice, page 50, Merguez, page 76, Mexican Chorizo, page 84,
and Spanish Chorizo, page 74*

Jalapeño peppers are tiny, bright-green, and quite hot. They aren't the hottest peppers on the market, but they pack a punch. Here, mustard and mayonnaise help smooth out the flavors. Use this sauce as an appetizer dip for grilled sausages, or use it on sausage sandwiches and burgers. It keeps well in the refrigerator for a month or two, as long as it is stored in a container with a tight lid.

½ cup mustard

½ cup mayonnaise

2 jalapeño peppers, minced

1 tablespoon jalapeño jelly

1 clove garlic, minced

1 tablespoon freshly squeezed lime juice

⅛ teaspoon freshly ground white pepper

1. Combine all of the ingredients in a small bowl and blend well with a wire whisk.

2. Store, covered, in the refrigerator for up to 2 months.

SPICY BEER SAUCE

MAKES 1 CUP | PREP TIME: 10 MINUTES | COOK TIME: 15 MINUTES

Good with Garlic Sausage, page 57, Bacon Cheeseburger Sausage, page 49, Beef Bangers, page 65, and Fresh Kielbasa, page 56

All sausage lovers know that these meats are delicious with a cold beer. But have you ever thought of making a spicy sauce from beer to serve with the sausages? Use your favorite variety in this easy recipe. A dark lager will make the sauce spicier, while an American lager will be lighter. Pilsner beer will add a bit of a malt zing, while brown ale brings a nutty, caramel flavor. Just be careful not to cook this recipe for too long or it may become bitter.

1¼ cups beer

⅓ cup minced onion

¼ cup beef stock

1 tablespoon honey

1 chipotle chile pepper in adobo
   sauce, minced

1 tablespoon apple cider vinegar

½ teaspoon salt

1. In a medium saucepan, combine the beer, onion, beef stock, honey, chile, apple cider vinegar, and salt.

2. Cook over medium heat, stirring frequently, until the sauce reduces by ⅓, about 10 to 15 minutes.

3. Let the sauce cool and then strain the sauce or blend it together.

4. Store in the refrigerator, in a tightly closed container, for up to 3 weeks.

SWEET CHUTNEY

MAKES 1½ CUPS | PREP TIME: 10 MINUTES | COOK TIME: 15 MINUTES

Good with Currywurst 2.0, page 61, Mexican Chorizo, page 84,

Spanish Chorizo, page 74, Bockwurst, page 58, Weisswurst, page 60,

Garlic Sausage, page 57, and Ćevapi, page 85

Chutney is a sweet-and-spicy sauce from India that is made with lots of fruit, vinegar, and spices. It is traditionally served with curry dishes, but it makes a great sauce for sausages. You can use whatever spices you'd like in this recipe. The classic spices for chutney include ginger, cardamom, cinnamon, curry powder, and mustard seeds. And the classic fruit is mango.

3 mangos, peeled and chopped

1 small onion, chopped

1 tablespoon grated fresh ginger

½ cup honey

2 tablespoons brown sugar

⅓ cup apple cider vinegar

2 teaspoons curry powder

1 teaspoon cinnamon

½ teaspoon salt

¼ teaspoon ground cardamom

¼ teaspoon mustard seeds

⅛ teaspoon cayenne pepper

1. In a large saucepan, combine all of the ingredients.

2. Bring to a boil over medium-high heat, then reduce the heat to low and simmer until the mangos and onion soften and the sauce is thick. Stir often while cooking.

3. Decant the sauce into a large jar, cool with the lid off for 1 hour, then cover and refrigerate for up to 3 weeks.

SMOKY ROOT-BEER SAUCE

SERVES 4 | PREP TIME: 10 MINUTES | COOK TIME: 40 MINUTES

Good with Rosemary-Lamb Sausage, page 46, Classic Pub Bangers, page 64, fresh Kielbasa, page 56, Bratwurst, page 59, and Marylebone Sausage, page 70

Root beer is a soda drink that was originally made from sassafras or sarsaparilla. It is sweet and slightly spicy, with a rich taste that makes it a fabulous base for our sauce. Smoked paprika gives this sauce more flavor, pairing nicely with the sweet root beer. Serve as an appetizer dip for grilled sausages, or use it as a spread on sandwiches.

2 tablespoons peanut or safflower oil

1 onion, finely chopped

2 garlic cloves, minced

2 cups root beer

3 tablespoons light brown sugar

1 tablespoon molasses

1 tablespoon freshly squeezed lemon juice

1 teaspoon smoked paprika

½ teaspoon salt

⅛ teaspoon cayenne pepper

1. In a large saucepan over medium heat, heat the peanut oil and add the onion and garlic.

2. Cook and stir until the onion starts to caramelize, about 20 to 30 minutes. Remove the pan from the heat.

3. Carefully add the root beer, brown sugar, molasses, lemon juice, paprika, salt, and cayenne and stir.

4. Return the pan to the heat and cook until the sauce is reduced to 1 cup.

5. Cool for 1 hour, then store covered in the refrigerator for up to 3 weeks.

HORSERADISH CREAM

MAKES 1 CUP | PREP TIME: 10 MINUTES

Good with Bacon Cheeseburger Sausage, page 49, Classic Pub Bangers, page 64, Mexican Chorizo, page 84, Spanish Chorizo, page 74, Sweet Italian Sausage, page 77, and Vietnamese Chicken Sausage, page 89

Horseradish is a root vegetable that is very strong and spicy. You can buy it fresh, but it's a lot easier to buy prepared horseradish. It comes grated in a jar and packed in vinegar. Don't buy horseradish mustard for this recipe; that's not the version we need. The spicy horseradish is combined with whipped cream, sour cream, and mayonnaise for a smooth sauce with quite a kick.

⅓ cup heavy cream

¼ cup prepared horseradish

2 tablespoons sour cream

2 tablespoons mayonnaise

1 tablespoon apple cider vinegar

½ teaspoon salt

⅛ teaspoon freshly ground white pepper

1. In a small bowl, beat the heavy cream until stiff peaks form.

2. Fold in the horseradish, sour cream, mayonnaise, apple cider vinegar, salt, and pepper.

3. Cover and store in the refrigerator for up to 4 days.

CARAMELIZED-ONION KETCHUP

MAKES 1 CUP | PREP TIME: 10 MINUTES | COOK TIME: 1 HOUR

Good with Tomato Sausage, page 69, Bockwurst, page 58, Bratwurst, page 59, Merguez, page 76, Sweet Italian Sausage, page 77, Beef Bangers, page 65, and Bacon Cheeseburger Sausage, page 49

Ketchup is a classic sauce that's good with any sausage, and here we spice it up a bit by adding caramelized onions. When cooked for a long time, the sugars in the onion break up into smaller molecules, causing the onions to become very sweet and slightly smoky. The onions also get very tender, which makes them the perfect addition to this smooth sauce. Store in the refrigerator for up to 3 days.

2 tablespoons butter

1 tablespoon olive oil

1 onion, finely chopped

½ teaspoon salt

½ cup ketchup

1 tablespoon tomato paste

1 tablespoon honey

1 tablespoon apple cider vinegar

½ teaspoon smoked paprika

1. In a medium skillet over medium heat, melt the butter and olive oil.

2. Add the onion and cook, stirring frequently, for 10 minutes. Then reduce the heat to low and cook, stirring often, until the onions are deep golden brown. This should take 30 to 40 minutes.

3. Add the salt, ketchup, tomato paste, honey, apple cider vinegar, and paprika and bring to a simmer.

4. Simmer the mixture for 10 minutes, or until the flavors blend.

5. Cool at room temperature for 1 hour, then cover and refrigerate.

CHILI SAUCE

MAKES 1 CUP | PREP TIME: 10 MINUTES

Good with Beef Bangers, page 65, Fresh Kielbasa, page 56, Ćevapi, page 85,
Cumberland Sausage, page 67, Lincolnshire Sausage, page 66, Lorne, page 68,
and Tomato Sausage, page 69

Chili sauce can be purchased from the store, of course, but there's nothing like your own homemade version. This combines ketchup with mustard, vinegar, and lots of spices. You can make your chili sauce mild or spicy, depending on the ingredients you use. If you like a lot of spice, use habanero chiles. If you want a milder sauce, use jalapeños. Mix this sauce with some sour cream or mayonnaise for an appetizer dip.

½ cup ketchup

2 tablespoons grainy mustard

2 tablespoons white vinegar

2 tablespoons brown sugar

1 tablespoon tomato paste

1 tablespoon honey

1 jalapeño or habanero chile, minced

1 garlic clove, minced

¼ teaspoon onion powder

¼ teaspoon ground allspice

⅛ teaspoon freshly ground white pepper

1. Put all of the ingredients in a medium bowl and blend with a wire whisk until combined.

2. Store in the refrigerator, tightly covered, for up to 1 week.

Glossary

Should you decide to seek out more advanced books on the topic of sausage making, it may be helpful to familiarize yourself with some of the technical terms you may encounter. Here is a list of the most common ones, briefly defined.

amino acids: the building blocks of protein.

auger: the corkscrew-shaped piece of the assembly on an electrically powered meat grinder that draws meat forward toward the blade as the motor operates.

binders: substances that help sausage ingredients stick together; common examples include milk powder, caseinate, egg, gelatin, flour, and starch.

Bloom number: a measure of the strength of gelatin; a higher Bloom number indicates greater binding power for a given amount (typical values range from 125 to 250).

botulism: a potentially fatal foodborne illness that results from improperly handled sausage, caused by bacteria that thrive in anaerobic (oxygen-free) environments—particularly a problem when sausages are improperly cured.

brine: a solution of salt and/or sugar dissolved in liquid. Helps meat retain moisture when cooked.

carrageenan: a gum derived from seaweed that thickens and gelatinizes mixtures when heated. Also helps sausage retain moisture.

caseinate: a type of milk protein used to help emulsify ingredients.

caul fat: a type of intestinal fat that can be used as a casing.

chimney starter: a device that helps easily and safely light charcoal for a smoker or grill.

cold smoking: smoking that occurs below temperatures of 200°F, which helps preserve and flavor meat.

collagen: a substance that makes up the connective tissue responsible for linking muscle fibers together. It breaks down into gelatin when exposed to heat, turning the texture pleasantly slick.

comminution: the process of cutting meat into smaller pieces.

conditioning: for cured sausages, a period of time after stuffing during which the sausages are left at a specific range of temperatures to dry.

curing: the process of preserving meat through drying, smoking, or adding certain substances—in sausage making, typically nitrates or nitrites—or any combination of the three.

emulsification: the binding of meat, fat, and liquid together.

exudate: the solution that forms between meat proteins and salt on cut surfaces when exposed to heat and mechanical action.

farce: a combination of protein and liquid characterized by a sticky texture.

fermentation: a process by which beneficial bacteria are intentionally allowed to multiply (and harmful bacteria are destroyed) in a food product under controlled conditions—such as temperature, humidity, acidity, and time—in order to transform its flavor and texture.

fillers: ingredients used to help cut down on the amount of meat needed to make sausage, but can also contribute to unique texture. Examples include bread crumbs, buckwheat groats, flour, rice, and oats.

headcheese: a type of large sausage traditionally made from meat obtained from a boiled hog's head.

hot smoking: smoking that occurs at temperatures above 200°F, which flavors and cooks the meat at the same time.

konjac gum: a type of calorie-free gum derived from the root of a plant that is an exceptionally effective thickener—10 times more effective than cornstarch.

myoglobin: a compound found in meat that is responsible for its red hue; the more myoglobin meat has, the darker it appears.

nitrate/nitrite: a type of salt used to cure sausages, colloquially known as "pink salt" for the color it gives the meat; also prevents botulism.

non-resinous wood: also known as hardwood, the best choice for smoking. Popular varieties include apple, cherry, hickory, oak, pecan, and mesquite.

offal: a polite term for organ meats (pronounced "OH-ful" and not "awful").

pH: a logarithmic (squished down) scale measuring acidity that runs from 1 to 14. A lower pH indicates more acidity; a higher pH indicates less acidity (and more alkalinity). Water has a "neutral" pH of 7; most meat sits just below that.

resinous wood: wood from trees that have soft bark, such as pine. Avoid using these for smoking, as they will impart a bitter taste.

rusk: a type of filler made by moistening flour, then baking and grinding it.

saltpeter: another name for potassium nitrate, a curing salt.

show meat: sausages that contain unique visual features, such as whole chunks of fat, nuts, or peppers.

souse: a type of headcheese that incorporates vinegar.

textured vegetable protein: a meat substitute with a neutral flavor and high protein content that is made from soybeans, typically used to make vegetarian sausage.

transglutaminase: also known as "meat glue," this substance is used to bind meat from different animals together.

water activity: a measure of how much water in a sausage can be used by bacteria (good and bad) to grow and multiply on a scale from 0 to 1. Water rates a 1 on this scale; a perfectly dry surface is a 0. Fresh meat comes in at 0.99, salami at 0.87, on average.

water-holding capacity: the degree to which a type of meat can absorb water; fresher meat with higher pH retains more moisture.

xanthan gum: a gum made by exposing sugars to a specific strain of bacteria that helps prevent emulsions from breaking.

References

Aidells, Bruce. *Bruce Aidells' Complete Sausage Book: Recipes From America's Premium Sausage Maker*. New York: Ten Speed Press, 2000.

Farr, Ryan. *Sausage Making: The Definitive Guide with Recipes*. San Francisco: Chronicle Books, 2014.

Marianski, Stanley, and Adam Marianski. *Home Production of Quality Meats and Sausages*. Seminole, FL: Bookmagic, 2010.

Peery, Susan M., and Charles G. Reavis. *Home Sausage Making: How-To Techniques for Making and Enjoying 100 Sausages at Home*. North Adams, MA: Storey Publishing, 2003.

Peisker, James, and James Carter. *Homemade Sausage: Recipes and Techniques to Grind, Stuff, and Twist Artisanal Sausage at Home*. Beverly, MA: Quarry Books, 2016.

Resources

MEAT, POULTRY, AND SEAFOOD

Bell & Evans. BellandEvans.com

Copper River Salmon. CopperRiverSalmon.org

D'Artagnan Foods. DArtagnan.com

Heritage Foods USA. HeritageFoodsUSA.com

Louisiana Crawfish Company. LACrawfish.com

Mary's Chickens. MarysChickens.com

Niman Ranch. NimanRanch.com

Omaha Steaks. OmahaSteaks.com

SAUSAGE-MAKING RESOURCES

Amazing Ribs. AmazingRibs.com

Franco's Famous Sausage Making. SausageMaking.org

Meats and Sausages. MeatsAndSausages.com

The Smoke Ring. TheSmokeRing.com

SPICES AND SEASONINGS

Kalustyan's. Kalustyans.com

Morton & Bassett. MortonBassett.com

Patel Brothers. PatelBros.com

Recipe Index

Index

Acknowledgments

I'd like to thank Meg Ilasco, my managing editor, for making this project possible. It has been a pleasure working with you, and I am sure that this cookbook is only one of many more to come. And, of course, I'd be remiss in not giving my heartfelt thanks to all of the hardworking people at Callisto Media and the mighty team of freelancers who made sure that this book made it through every step of the production process on time.

Most importantly, thank you to my vegetarian boyfriend, Deepak Venkatachalam, who was a way better sport than he had to be while I was constantly grinding meat during testing—and filling up our refrigerator and freezer with meats and sausages of all kinds for weeks on end. One of these days, I will write a book about vegetarian sausages, just for you.

About the Author

WILL BUDIAMAN is a New York City–based freelance writer and recipe developer. He is a graduate of the International Culinary Center, and is currently working full-time as a recipe editor. Previously, he served as a recipe tester for Maple, as a web producer for *Bon Appétit* and *Epicurious*, and as a recipe editor at *The Daily Meal*, where he ran the test kitchen. He has written five other cookbooks, including two books about barbecue. For more information or to purchase his other titles, visit WillBudiaman.com.

CPSIA information can be obtained
at www.ICGtesting.com
Printed in the USA
BVHW01s0158251117
501165BV00001B/1/P